Zulu Battle Piece: Isandhlwana, 1879

Photograph by J.H.L.

Zulu Battle Piece: Isandhlwana, 1879

With New Illustrations and First Hand Accounts

ILLUSTRATED

Sir Reginald Coupland

With Eyewitness Accounts by

Sir H. Smith-Dorrien, and G. Hamilton-Browne

LEONAUR

Zulu Battle Piece: Isandhlwana, 1879
With New Illustrations and First Hand Accounts
By Sir Reginald Coupland
With Eyewitness Accounts by
Sir H. Smith-Dorrien and G. Hamilton-Browne

ILLUSTRATED

FIRST EDITION

Leonaur is an imprint of Oakpast Ltd
Copyright in this form © 2023 Oakpast Ltd

ISBN: 978-1-916535-06-0 (hardcover)
ISBN: 978-1-916535-07-7 (softcover)

http://www.leonaur.com

Publisher's Notes

The views expressed in this book are not necessarily
those of the publisher.

Contents

THE ZULU MONUMENT, ISANDLWANA BY J.H.L.

Preface

Nearly seventy years have passed (1948), since Isandhlwana, but, except on one or two minor points which will probably never be settled, there is sufficient evidence to reconstruct the course of the battle with reasonable certainty, (1) There are detailed official reports most of which are reproduced in the blue-books: an examination of the files at the Public Record Office shows that nothing of importance was omitted from the published text. Another official source is the *Narrative of Field Operations Connected with the Zulu War*, prepared at the War Office soon after the event and published in 1881. (2) A few eye-witness accounts by survivors of the battle and the defence of Rorke's Drift, other than those given in the official reports, have been preserved. Some Zulu evidence has also survived.

When I visited the battlefield last winter, I interviewed a Zulu over eighty years old, who had taken part in the fight as a warrior of the Nkobamakosi regiment. (3) Of contemporary unofficial narratives the most valuable is Norris Newman's *In Zululand with the British* (London, 1880) He was the only newspaper correspondent with the British troops at that stage of the campaign, and, though fortunately he was not present at the battle, he was on the ground a few hours after it was over. Of other books written at the time, the most important, though not the most objective, is Lt-Col. E. Durnford's *A Soldier's Life and Work in South Africa* (London, 1882). (4) There is very little new evidence though some new interpretation, in the later secondary authorities. The most recent and detailed of these is the

Hon. Gerald French's *Lord Chelmsford and the Zulu War* (London, 1939).

R. C.

Woofton Hill,
May, 1948.

Isandlwana view by J.H.L.

THE BATTLE

OF Isandlwana

BRITISH INFANTRY SQUARE

Prelude

1

The Zulus are the most famous of all the native peoples of South Africa, and they owe their fame to their military record. None of the other well-known Bantu folk—Basuto, Pondo, Swazi, Matabele—fought as the Zulus fought. For sixty or seventy years their armies were a constant menace to the peace and safety of their neighbours, and it was not only other black men who learned to their cost how dangerous they were. Twice in that period the Zulus were at open war with white men, with the Boers in 1838, with the British in 1879. Both of those wars ended, as they were bound to end, in overwhelming Zulu defeat; but both of them began with Zulu victories so complete, so decisive at the moment, so grimly dramatic, that they will never be forgotten. The scene of the second victory was Isandhlwana.

The Zulu power was the creation of King Chaka, a despot of unusual brutality whose career of conquest earned him the title of the 'Black Napoleon.' Before his day the Zulus were only one minor Bantu clan of the many which for generations past had been drifting south-eastwards from the tropical heart of Africa. By the end of the fifteenth century this great race-migration, had reached the Zambesi valley. By the end of the eighteenth, it had come up against the sea along the east coast of South Africa. It was soon after that, at about the time of Waterloo, that Chaka became King of the Zulus and began to attack and subdue the neighbouring tribes.

Hitherto intertribal warfare, though as chronic a feature of savage as of civilised society, had not, it seems, been very destructive. Defeated tribes had lived to fight another day. Their conquerors had been content with submission and tribute. But Chaka fought to destroy. As far as he could, he blotted his victims out. He carried off the women and the cattle: He drafted the surviving men and boys into the Zulu Army. By 1823 he was undisputed master of the whole area which now constitutes the Province of Natal.

The Xosas, Pondos and other 'Kaffir' tribes had been pushed southwards down the coast. The Basutos, soon to be consolidated by their great chief, Moshesh, had found refuge in the little mountain country that bears their name. The Matabele, led by Mosilikatzi, an offshoot of the Zulus and no less militant, had retreated to the 'high *veld*' of the interior. That was the limit of Chaka's triumphs. In 1826 his brother, Dingaan, murdered him and seized the throne.

Dingaan, though not much less cruel than Chaka, was not at heart a warrior. He maintained the Zulu Army, but he did not launch it on new campaigns of conquest. The outstanding war of his reign, the war with the Boers, began, it is true, with a flagrant act of aggression on his part. None the less, it was, in the strictest sense, a defensive war. It was one of the many conflicts, which had inevitably resulted from the expansion of European settlement northwards from the Cape.

If the Dutch and British colonists had had to deal only with the earlier inhabitants of South Africa, the aboriginal Bushmen and the Hottentots, no wars worth the name would have been fought. Relatively few and feeble, those primitive peoples would have been brushed aside by the immigrants from oversea as easily as the aborigines of Australia. But the European invasion from the south coincided, as it happened, with the Bantu invasion from the north; and, since the Bantu were sturdy and prolific fighting folk, far outnumbering the whites, the upshot was a long-drawn-out struggle all along the shifting line of contact between the rival claimant to the soil of South Africa.

They met first on the north-east frontier of Cape Colony.

From 1779 to 1781 the Dutch border-farmers were engaged in trying to thrust back beyond the Great Fish River the vanguard of the Bantu tribes already pushing down across the belt of grassland between the mountains and the sea. The conflict thus begun inevitably continued.

On the one hand the white frontiersmen, seeking new land for stock farming, strove to extend their area of settlement. On the other hand, the tribes were forced forward into the same debatable country, partly by the growth of their own population, partly, as at the time of Zulu conquest, by pressure from their rear. Between 1781 and 1830 there were seven more so-called 'Kaffir Wars.'

From about 1835 onwards the area of contact and conflict between white and black was vastly enlarged by the Great Trek. That historic exodus of discontented Boers from Cape Colony, seeking to live their own old way of life uncontrolled by what they regarded as the mistaken and meddlesome humanity of the British Government, went fast and far. ('Boer,' which means 'farmer,' was the name given in the nineteenth century to the Afrikaners of the inland Republics). Already by 1838 some of the country between the Orange and the Vaal, soon to be known as the Orange Free State, had been occupied, and the more venturous spirits had pressed on across the 'high *veld*' beyond the Vaal.

Over most of the great inland plateau the Bantu population was not numerous, but at three points the Trekkers came into contact with compact and formidable tribes. On the eastern border of the Free State were the Basutos, with whom there was constant indecisive fighting for the possession of a stretch of good land below the mountains, only ended when in 1868, at the aged Moshesh's request, Basutoland was annexed by the British Government at the Cape. Beyond the Vaal the 'Trek-Boers' were confronted northwards by the Matabele and eastwards by the Zulus. These were more powerful enemies than the Basutos, more addicted and inured to warfare, better disciplined, more ruthless.

The Boers as a whole numbered only a few thousand, the

'commandos' that took the field only a few hundred. Courage alone—and they had plenty of it—would not have availed to give them the mastery. They owed it to their muskets, their horses, and their tactics. They were first-rate marksmen. Hunting game on horseback, especially running buck, had been their daily occupation from boyhood up. On the open *veld* they could always keep their distance from native forces unmounted and armed only with *assegais* and a few antiquated and often ill-aimed muskets: they could ride within range, shoot without wasting shot, and gallop off. Their danger lay in broken country and at night If they could be caught by surprise at close quarters, numbers and *assegais* would tell.

But against that they had devised a most effective method of defence, the *laager*. They drew up the big ox-wagons which formed their moving habitation in a great circle, chained their wheels together, and stuffed the gaps with brushwood. Inside the oxen and horses were tethered. The tilted wagons served both as tents for the women and children and as a battlement for the men in the event of attack.

Against the Matabele this offensive and defensive technique was combined with striking success. In the autumn of 1836, a Boer trek-party was attacked by some 5,000 Matabele at Vegkop, not far south of the Vaal. There were only forty men, but they had had time to form a *laager*, and their womenfolk, as brave as they, were ready to keep them supplied with bullets and powder and to help reload their guns. For several hours on end the Matabele flung themselves with desperate bravery against the wagons, and it was not till about one-third of their number had been shot down that at last they withdrew. The Boer casualties were only two men killed and a dozen wounded by flung *assegais*.

At the beginning of 1837 the Boers retaliated with a sharp surprise attack on the Matabele settlement at Mosega. At midsummer the Matabele suffered heavily in a fierce battle with the Zulus. In November they were finally defeated by the Boers. Leaving their wagons in the Marico valley, a commando of 135 men rode over the *veld* for fifty miles till they met the Matabele

Army not far from Mosilikatzi's royal *kraal* at Kapain. It was several thousand strong, but the little troop of Boer horsemen manoeuvred so skilfully and shot so well that after a nine-day running fight the Matabele abandoned their capital and some 7,000 head of cattle and fled away northwards.

Those three reverses in one year were enough, and Mosilikatzi decided to leave the 'high *veld*' to his enemies and make a home for his people north of the Limpopo. There they remained for over fifty years, a terror to their native neighbours, but safe beyond the malarious Limpopo lowlands from the intrusive white man. It was not till 1890 that the founders of Rhodesia occupied Mashonaland next door. In 1893 came the last Matabele war, in 1896 their last revolt

There remained the Zulus. Till 1837 Dingaan had nothing to fear. He had disposed of the Matabele, Swazis and Basutos and the tribes of Kaffraria might be in sore need of land, but none of them dreamed of seeking it within the limits of a Zulu realm that stretched from Delagoa Bay to the Umzimkulu River and from the Drakensberg mountains to the sea. But in the summer of 1837, he learned that not a few Boers had parted from their comrades on the 'high *veld*' and were driving their creaking wagons towards the rocky passes of the Drakensberg overlooking his Natal.

In November their leader, Piet Retief, was so bold as to come in person to Dingaan's royal *kraal* at Umgungundhlovu, with only four or five companions, to solicit a grant of land, Dingaan conceded it on condition that the Boers would save him the trouble of recovering some cattle which Sikonyela, an audacious chief from the Drakensberg area, had stolen from the royal herds. He was soon to learn what this concession meant. As soon as the news got back to the 'high *veld*,' a host of Trekkers, their previous hesitation overcome, came streaming down the passes into the beautiful well-watered countryside of northern Natal.

By the end of the month 'there were close on a thousand wagons spread out along the streams that run into the upper Tugela.' This was bad enough news, and on its heels came the report of the Marico fighting and the astonishing prowess which the Boers had displayed against the Matabele.

Finally, towards the end of January, 1838, Dingaan learned that Retief was on his way back to Umgungundhlovu bringing the cattle, which he had recovered from Sikonyela by a ruse, and intending, no doubt, to claim the execution of his bond. He had some seventy white men with him—a formidable force in battle but not too strong to be trapped. So Dingaan decided to scotch the dangerous snake that was coiling its way into his dominions.

Having concealed some thousands of his warriors in the many huts that surrounded his own residence and place of audience, he received his visitors with friendly dignity and, after a day or two of negotiations, during which martial displays were staged by Boers and Zulus alike, he set his mark to a deed granting all the land between the Tugela and the Umzimkulu to the Boers. Thereupon he invited them to come unarmed to a farewell beer-drinking. They came, and, at a sudden order, Dingaan's warriors fell on their guests and slew them all (February 6, 1838).

Then, before the news of the massacre could reach them, an *impi* (army) was dispatched to wipe out the whole body of Boer immigrants. Their camps lay widely spread among the streams that feed the upper Tugela. So sure were they that Retief had come to an amicable understanding with Dingaan that even the usual *laagers* had been dispensed with or left incomplete. They were ill-protected, therefore, and quite unaware of danger when the Zulus fell upon them in the middle of the night.

The more advanced encampments were overwhelmed. Most of those set farther back got news of the attack in time to strengthen their defences. Sporadic fighting lasted till dawn and on into the morning. When at last the Boers were able to collect their scattered forces to take the offensive, the Zulus withdrew. They had slaughtered 41 Boer men, about 240 Boer women and children, and some 200 of their coloured servants.

More blows followed. In April the Boers attempted a counter-attack. A double commando, nearly 350 men in all, crossed the Buffalo to deal with the Zulus as the Matabele had been dealt with. But they were caught by the Zulus in broken rocky ground, the commandos were separated, one of them was surrounded, and the whole force was sent flying back to the safety of the *laagers*. Though the casualties were not so heavy, this defeat at Italeni in open battle was more discouraging than either of the previous disasters which had been inflicted by surprise. About the same time another *impi* swept, down to the coast.

Many of the white residents at Fort Natal (soon to be known as Durban) had sought safety southwards, and the little party that remained, including several fugitive English and American missionaries, would have been massacred but for the timely arrival of a small coasting ship. From its crowded deck the refugees watched the Zulus pillaging the township for nine days. On the tenth they retired with their loot.

Cut off from the sea, the triumphant Zulus in front, the mountains at their back, the isolated immigrants in northern Natal could scarcely have been charged with cowardice if they had abandoned the enterprise and trekked back to the 'high *veld*.' A section of them did. But some 3,500 stood their ground, closely *laagered*, and waited for better times. Their courage was soon rewarded. Towards the end of that same year (1838) Andries Pretorius, ablest and most trusted of the Boer leaders, (Pretoria was named after him), rode down from the 'high *veld*' with a party of fighting men and took command of the united Boer forces. Nearly 500 strong, they crossed the Buffalo again, and on December 15 they formed *laager* in a strong position, protected on one side by a deep-flowing river and on another by a broad ravine.

Next day, a Sunday, the Zulus in great force attacked the open flanks. For more than two hours they strove with their usual desperate valour to penetrate the ring of wagons. Then the gates were opened and the Boer horsemen with no less courage rode straight at the wavering Zulu ranks. They broke and fled. It was a crushing defeat. Some 3,000 of their warriors, it was reckoned, had been killed. Their bodies lay thick, wrote an observer, as 'pumpkins on a rich soil.' Some of them were caught at the edge of the river. 'The water looked like a pool of blood: whence came the name of Blood River.' For the Boers it was even more striking proof than the Marico battle that their military technique was irresistible if properly applied. Not a single man of them was killed and only three were wounded.

The victors at once pressed on to Umgungundhlovu. They found it deserted. On the 'hill of execution' the remains of the bodies of Retief and his companions lay where they had been thrown. In Retief's knapsack was the deed of cession. Blood River had made it valid, Dingaan could not now contest the Boers' occupation of Natal, and, having learned his lesson, he might be expected not to meddle with them there if they left him alone in Zululand. But his power was not broken, and, when a chance presented itself of making an end him, the Boers seized it.

About a year after Blood River, Dingaan's brother, Panda, crossed the Tugela frontier with a host of followers and, encamping near Port Natal, offered the Boers his alliance. The offer was accepted, and early in 1840 a Boar commando, 400 strong, led again by Pretorius, and a powerful Zulu *impi* advanced into Zululand on parallel lines. The Zulus were the first to join battle, with their kinsfolk: they won a decisive victory and Dingaan fled to the north where presently he was killed in a fight with the Swazi. Meantime, with a solemn salute of guns, Pretorius had proclaimed Panda King of the Zulus.

2

Nearly forty years passed before there was another Zulu war. This time it was not Boer commandos with whom the Zulus fought, but a British Army.

Till 1843 there was no contact between the British Government and Zululand. The Governor of Cape Colony was far away at Cape Town. Between the northeast frontier of the Colony and Natal lay the coastal belt, 200 miles long, a patchwork of tribal territories not finally annexed to the Cape till

1894. It is safe to say that the British Government would have made no northward move if the Great Trek had not forced its hand. But the difficulties and dangers involved in that rupture of the natural unity of South Africa were soon apparent. Were the Trekkers, still *de jure* British subjects, to be permitted to establish independent Republics, free on the one hand to negotiate with foreign powers and on the other hand to deal as they chose with their native neighbours whatever might be the reaction on the native neighbours of Cape Colony?

After a period of hesitation two forward step were taken. In 1843, Natal was annexed, partly to protect the local tribes from Boer aggression, partly for the same strategic reason which impelled the annexation of St Lucia Bay forty years later. Next, in 1848, the country between the Orange and the Vaal was annexed as the Orange River Sovereignty. But this forward movement was soon reversed. In 1852 the British Government recognised the domestic freedom of the Transvaal Boers, and in 1854 the Orange River Sovereignty became the Orange Free State.

But the virtual independence conceded in the interior was withheld on the sea-board. Natal, from which most of the original Trekkers had resentfully withdrawn after 1843, remained a British Colony. Thus, it was not a Boer President and his *Volksraad* that ruled the land ceded by Dingaan but a British Lieutenant-Governor and his Council.

Between 1855 and 1875 it might have seemed as if the complex of British Colonies, Boer Republics and Bantu tribal states had acquired some stability. The intermittent conflict with the Basutos did not spread, and it was ended in 1868. After the defeat of the Gaikas in 1851 there was not another 'Kaffir War' till 1877. Even the Zulus seemed to have taken to heart the lesson of Dingaan's fall. Panda was a weak and unwarlike king, and in Theophilus Shepstone the Natal Government had found an agent who acquired a most remarkable personal influence over the Zulu people. It might almost have been said that their trusted '*Somsteu*' ruled them more than Panda. But this outward peace masked a growing tension. Forces were at work that were bound, sooner or later, to bring about another explosion.

The first and greatest of these was land hunger. The Bantu are a virile, prolific race; and in the coastal belt, especially towards its southern end, the growth of population was fast outstripping the resources of the land. Primitive husbandry, exhaustion of soil, excess of cattle, and erosion made matters worse. A serious drought—and the spectre of drought has always haunted South Africa's agrarian economy—meant widespread famine, and more and more tribesmen were forced to seek work and sustenance away from home, on farms within the colonial frontier or as far afield as Kimberley when, the diamond field was opened there in 1869. The land-hunger of the natives could have been satisfied, for a time at any rate, in the areas they inhabited if the intrusive white man had not also been land-hungry. This was not due in their case to pressure of population: the number of colonists, British and Afrikaner, was still very small. (The Afrikaans word *Afrikaner* is the modem version of 'Dutch-speaking South African.' *Afrikander* to the English form).

But most of such land as was not too dry to live on was quite unfit for intensive agriculture: hence the size of the average farm was far greater than in countries blessed with better soil and climate: custom fixed it at 6,000 acres and it was often twice that or more. But there was another less natural reason for land-scarcity. Huge tracts were bought up by greedy speculators who held them undeveloped against the day when the coming of roads and railways would greatly enhance their market value. Thus, black land-hunger was confronted by white land-hunger, and the blacks, so far from being able to expand into white areas except as labourers, began steadily to lose their own lands to the whites.

By 1870 the whites' acquisition of land in native territories had been checked and controlled in the coastal belt and on the Basuto border, and though the artificial land-scarcity caused by speculation was nowhere worse than in Natal, it had not yet made trouble with its Zulu neighbours. The native problem in Natal at this time was primarily an internal problem. The colonists numbered less than 50,000. The native inhabitants, mostly

Zulus who had lived there since the time of Chaka or sought refuge there from the cruelties of Dingaan's reign, numbered over 300,000. Yet the whites, as individuals or land-companies, owned five-sixths of the land; and many of the blacks were forced either to live on sufferance on land to which they had no tide or to seek service on the white men's farms or in their towns. But this internal problem had not so far created any dangerous interracial tension. The Zulu proletariat preferred to be cramped for living room in Natal than to be pushed back within the scope of Zulu despotism.

As far as Natal was concerned the traditional reason for such a renewal of strife with the Zulus did not operate. Beyond the frontier fixed by Dingaan's cession the acquisition of land by white men was effectively discouraged except for such special purposes as mission-stations. And there was no doubt where the frontier lay. It was plainly marked by the Buffalo River from its source in the mountains till it flowed into the Tugela and thence by the Tugela to the sea. It was otherwise on the Transvaal side of Zululand.

Here there were no simple physical features to determine the boundary of Chaka's heritage—the rivers ran across the shifting line of contact between the Zulus and the Boers—and, since the early days of the Great Trek, the Boers had been steadily encroaching on what became known as the 'disputed territory,' obtaining grazing rights from local chiefs, converting them by occupation into rights of ownership, building their farmhouses, treating the native inhabitants as their subjects.

It was an old story. Wherever civilised and uncivilised men had met, and not in Africa only, the former had pushed the frontier back, until the process was stopped or regularised by an effective government. Such a government was operating in the other three white polities into which South Africa had been divided, but not in the Transvaal. The farmers who made up most of the Volksraad—the elected one-chamber legislature—did not wish to interfere with the familiar process of expansion, and, if they had wished, they had not sufficient authority to do it. So, the process continued. It was, no doubt, inevitable; but, as long as it continued, interracial conflict, whether an endless sequence of local disputes or a large-scale revolt, was equally inevitable.

3

In the early 'seventies' the instability of the existing equipoise of white and black began to manifest itself beneath the peaceful surface. In Natal, especially, uneasiness deepened into anxiety, and anxiety into fear.

One reason for this was the acquisition of firearms by the natives. Hitherto the *assegai* and to a less extent the battle-axe and *knobkerry* had been their only weapons; but now a stream of cheap guns was flowing into Zululand and Swaziland from Delagoa Bay; and the natives of all tribes who were flocking to the diamond field were buying guns with their wages. They were of poor quality and their owners often proved poor marksmen; but the new weapon certainly increased to some extent the fighting power of the natives. To the white men, well aware that they had owed mainly to their firearms the victories they had won against overwhelming numbers, this development seemed highly dangerous.

Hence the sharpness of the Natal Government's dispute in 1873 with Langalibalele, a chief on their north-west border, over the registration of guns brought back from Kimberley by his tribesmen, and the severity and questionable justice with which they punished his contumacy: So unprecedented, indeed, were their proceedings that Colenso, Bishop of Natal, who was as earnest and forthright in his championship of native rights as in his controversy with his fellow-churchmen on the historical validity of the Pentateuch, was able to persuade the Secretary of State for the Colonies in far away Whitehall, to interfere and moderate the sentence.

The belief that they now had a weapon that put them on even terms with the white man may have had something to do with the growing restlessness that pervaded the whole Bantu world at this time; but the dominant cause was economic. It was a period of successive droughts. Vegetation withered. Cattle perished of hunger and thirst. The pressure on the overpopulated land increased, and with it the urge to seek more and better-watered land elsewhere. Intertribal scuffles and raids became more frequent. The black man's demeanour towards the whites seemed to be becoming less submissive, more defiant. Messages passed from chief to chief, but there is not sufficient evidence to make it certain that anything like a general conceited rising was being planned. Some observers thought so, and they had no doubt where the source and mainstay of the trouble lay. Whether they were right or not, there was unquestionably a change in Zululand. As the decade drew on, nervous Natalians became aware that Zulu militarism had not disappeared with Dingaan.

In 1873 King Panda died; but old age and feebleness of character had long made his kingship little more than formal. The real authority lay with his son Cetewayo who in 1856 had fought and killed his brother and in 1861 had been recognised as heir-apparent by the Natal Government. Similar recognition was sought on his accession. Shepstone was already a power in the land, and Cetewayo asked his 'father *Somsteu*' to come and install him on his throne.

After some hesitation Shepstone and his superiors agreed, and he took occasion at the coronation ceremony to hold discussions with the new King and his Council and to declare that the traditional evils of Zulu Government must be reformed. There must be no more arbitrary killing. Minor culprits must be fined, not put to death.

It is not on record that Cetewayo explicitly accepted these rules, but in any case, it was clear, before very long, that he had no intention of keeping them. Killing continued. In 1876 Cetewayo executed several young women for breaking the military marriage rules. But, save as a revelation of Cetewayo's disposition, there was no danger in these domestic cruelties to his white neighbours in Natal. The danger lay in the military system. Cetewayo had set himself to revive and perfect the fighting machine which Chaka had created.

Cᴇᴛᴇᴡᴀʏᴏ ᴄ. 1875

Its organisation was simple and efficient, All the young men of a certain age-group were drafted into regiments for their period of service. They spent it in the great barracks or military homesteads, housing several thousands, which stood on the king's own land in the neighbourhood of his royal *kraal*. The marriage of these young warriors was strictly regulated. They were normally mated with similar age-groups of young women, and it had been the rule in old days that they could not marry at all till they had 'washed their spears' in blood. The revival of this custom, which seems to have lapsed in Panda's time, was the most sinister feature of Cetewayo's regime.

The army was a formidable force. Mobilised for war, it numbered some 50,000 out of a total population of about 250,000. And it was at once the symbol and cement of Zulu nationhood. It was regimented by age, not by clan. At the great national ceremonies—such as those of seedtime and harvest—the Zulu people did not assemble in clans: they paraded as regiments. It was control of them that gave the king his power, made him the embodiment of national unity, and, since from Chaka's day the welfare of the nation meant first in every Zulu mind its military might, won for him, as their leader in war, an emotional fidelity far deeper at a crisis than any loyalty to clan or kin.

The strength of the army was not merely in its numbers. It was their discipline that had made the Zulus more comparable in fighting power with white men than any other Bantu folk, except perhaps the Matabele. The regiments were drilled and drilled until they moved like a machine. And by constant practice they had perfected a particular tactical technique.

The main body of the *impi* was drawn up in long lines, with regular intervals of two or three paces between each line and each man. The central section was called the Chest, the two wings the Left and Right Horns. In the rear was the reserve or Loins. As the *impi* advanced—and the Zulus always manoeuvred to attack—the Chest, at the appropriate time, slowed down its pace while the Horns were rapidly extended and, advancing at full speed, attempted to encircle both the enemy's flanks.

The warriors carried, besides their great ox-hide shields, at least two *assegais* each, a longer one to throw, a shorter one to stab with. It was the latter they mainly depended on. At a distance of about 70 yards, they launched the throwing *assegai* and then charged home with a weight and ferocity which no other natives could withstand. When their victims turned and fled, they found that the Horns had rounded their flanks and come together in their rear. Massacre ensued.

Such was the tradition banded down from Chaka's day. The discipline and technique would still be effective no doubt, against Bantu enemies, but it had not yet been fully tried out against white men. Partial encirclement seems to have been achieved at Italeni, but on other occasions the Boers, though relatively only a handful, had defeated them by the counter-technique of the *laager*. Encirclement was of no avail against an enemy protected on all sides. The last fierce rash with the stabbing *assegais* was halted by the steady musket-fire from the wagons.

In strategy as distinguished from tactics the Zulus shared with other tribes one great advantage over all white forces that were not mounted—superior mobility. They had no cavalry: though some of the horses taken from Piet Retief's ill-fated party were ridden by *indunas* for a time, the idea of fighting on horseback was soon dropped. But except on clean and fairly level ground the Zulus could move as fast as horses. They needed no roads. They had no baggage-trains. They carried their food and weapons with them. They could move in any direction, night or day, at a springy stride or lope, covering long distances without rest, crossing the roughest stoniest country, climbing the steepest hills. And with this mobility went a capacity for concealment.

Zululand is a good place to hide in. The grass often grows waist-high. Bush-covered valleys intersect the rolling downland. Gullies cut across the plains. The foothills of the mountains are strewn with rocks, and their sides pitted with caves. Such country made it possible for quite a large native force, if well enough disciplined, virtually to disappear from white men's eyes. It made it possible, too, for the Zulus to get to close quarters with an enemy—and that was their objective—before he was aware of it.

4

It was in the course of 1876 that the fear of Zulu militarism became acute. In the previous autumn the acting president of the Transvaal Republic had annexed a strip of land on the Pongolo River in flat defiance of Cetewayo's claim that none of the 'disputed territory' had ever been ceded; and, a few months later, taxes were forcibly collected from the Zulu inhabitants of the strip. To Sir Henry Bulwer, shrewd and cool-headed Lieutenant-Governor of Natal (1875-1880), it seemed as if the Boers were bent on a collision. But Cetewayo, with Shepstone at his elbow, declined the challenge.

The crisis passed; and in the meantime, the Boers were diverted from expansion on the Zulu border by their quarrel with Secocoeni, chief of the Bapedi, a small but well-armed tribe in the north-east Transvaal. Commandos were called out, but, fighting in mountainous country and deserted by their Swazi allies, they suffered a sharp defeat, withdrew, and presently dispersed. It was a humiliating episode and naturally it encouraged Cetewayo. He no longer hated and feared the Boers, it was reported: he hated and despised them.

The reaction to the Boer reverse was not confined to Zululand. It was felt as far away as London.

When Disraeli formed his second ministry in 1874, he brought back to the Colonial Office the man who had previously served under him and his predecessor, Derby, in that post. Lord Carnarvon was industrious, far-seeing and constructive, and he had gained prestige by his tactful superintendence of the federation of the British North American Colonies in 1867. He was quick to see that Sir George Grey had been right in pleading for a federal reunion of South Africa in 1859. But he failed to realist sufficiently that the federation of Canada had not been his doing. He had encouraged it, blessed it, smoothed its path to the statute-book; but it was the Canadians who had initiated the project and, after full discussion amongst themselves, had drafted the constitution.

There was no such spontaneous impulse in South Africa; Cape Colony shrank from sharing the cost and the risks of native policy with poorer and weaker neighbours. Natal and the Orange Free State were not against federation in principle, nor were the business-men, mostly English, who lived in the townships of the Transvaal. But the passion for independence which had carried them so far north in the days of the Trek still fired the hearts of most of the rural Boers. Clearly there were formidable obstacles on the road to federation, only to be overcome by time and patience. But Carnarvon was not deterred. In the spring of 1875, he appealed to South African opinion in a masterly dispatch in which he argued the case for federation and proposed a conference in South Africa on the Canadian model.

The reaction was unfavourable: the proposal, it was held, had come from the wrong side of the water. Nor was the situation eased by the eloquent speeches of the historian, Froude, who was sent by Carnarvon to preach the federal gospel to the unenlightened colonists. Carnarvon then convoked a conference in London (August 1876); but it was ill-attended and could do little.

At this moment came news of the defeat of the Transvaal Boers by Secocoeni. It had been known for some time past that the Republic was in a bad way. It was virtually bankrupt. Its able and ambitious President Burgers had less influence with the more independent-minded Boers than Paul Kruger. Its Volksraad was impotent to enforce the payment of taxes or to control the relations of white and black on the frontier. And now it seemed that the Republic was not strong enough to face the danger which—so its critics asserted—it had done its best to provoke.

Could anything but British influence and, in the last resort, British military force prevent Cetewayo from unleashing his *impis* to overwhelm the scattered farmsteads of the Transvaal? In this situation Carnarvon saw a new chance of carrying federation. He had already conceived the idea that, since the Cape was obdurate, it might be easier to begin building up a federation at the other end of the map.

And surely now a penniless and apparently defenceless Transvaal would be willing to accept provincial self-government in a federated British South Africa if the British flag brought with it British money and British troops? Shepstone, who had been summoned to London for the conference, was sent back with secret orders to annex the Republic if he found that a sufficient body of public opinion was prepared to acquiesce in it. At the same time Carnarvon invited Sir Bartle Frere to go out as Governor of Cape Colony and High Commissioner. He had chosen him, he wrote, 'as the statesman who seems to me most capable of carrying my scheme of confederation into effect.' and, when that 'great work' had been accomplished, he hoped he would stay on 'to bring the new machine into working order as the first Governor-General of the South African Dominion.'

It was a good choice. Frere was the most distinguished 'proconsul' of the day. A brilliant career in India had culminated is the Governorship of Bombay and membership of the Governor-General's Council On retirement he had served on the India Council in London, and in 1872-3 he had been sent on a mission to Zanzibar to negotiate with the *Sultan* a treaty for the abolition of the Arab slave trade. He was a man of the highest character, of first-rate intellect, and of great personal charm. How far he was himself to blame for the misfortune that was soon to overtake him will be considered in due course.

Within a fortnight of his landing at Cape Town, he heard that Shepstone had acted on his instructions and annexed the Transvaal. The almost furtive method of this *coup d'état* was indefensible, yet conceivably it might have been excused by its results. If a really generous financial settlement had at once been made and the fullest possible measure of domestic self-government at once conceded, and an experienced and diplomatic administrator sent to Pretoria to put such a settlement through, it is possible, even probable, that the majority of the population—no more than some 45,000 at the tine—would have tolerated the British flag.

But such a vigorous programme was inhibited by the weakness

of Shepstone and the incompetence of his successor in charge at Pretoria, by Carnarvon's failure to recognise the strength of the Boer's love of freedom, and, not least, by the parsimony of the Treasury which only granted a niggardly £100,000. So, the chance, if it was a chance, slipped away. The Union Jack hung somewhat limply at Pretoria till in 1881 it was hauled down.

It was soon evident to Frere that the uncertainty of the situation in the Transvaal, the resentment its annexation had aroused, and the continued opposition of his ministers at the Cape to 'interference from abroad' had made federation impracticable for the time being. So, he turned to consider the native question. It was, after all, the question which, for Carnarvon as for Grey, was the cardinal reason for trying to restore the breach made by the Trek in the political unity of South Africa. Only a single South African government could frame and enforce a uniform native policy and relieve British soldiers and taxpayers from the recurrent cost of native wars.

On the character of such a policy Frere had clear and large ideas. First, with a legitimate suspicion of German designs on South Africa, be held that all the coastland should be annexed, both east and west, up to the Portuguese frontiers. Secondly, none of the native polities should retain its independence. Their territorial integrity and their domestic system of government might be preserved, but, as with the Native States (as they were then called) in India, British authority must be 'paramount' and used to moderate barbarism, to prevent aggression, and to suppress the traffic in arms and alcohol.

> There is no escaping from the responsibility which has already been incurred, ever since the English flag was planted on the castle here. All our real difficulties have arisen, and still arise, from attempting to evade or shift the responsibility.

Unpalatable doctrine, no doubt, but incontestable.

The increasing restlessness which, as has been seen, pervaded black South Africa at the time of Frere's arrival at the Cape was an argument to his mind not for caution and delay but for rapid and decisive action. The longer, he thought, the issue of paramountcy remained unsettled, the stronger and more widespread would grow the nascent spirit of revolt among the tribes. He must have realised at the outset that his policy would probably involve to some extent, though not perhaps to a great extent, the use of force; and he was prepared to use it to obtain such a final settlement as could alone—he rightly believed—protect the natives from themselves and from their unlicensed white exploiters.

It was not Frere, however, who was responsible for the explosion which occurred within six months of his landing. In 1877 the drought throughout South Africa was unusually severe and protracted. Cattle-raiding led to intertribal fighting; and the resistance of the Galekas and the Gaikas to police intervention precipitated the ninth and last of the 'Kaffir Wars.' It began in August, 1877, and ended in June, 1878, in the complete defeat of the tribesmen and the subjection of Griqualand to the control of white magistrates. But that was not the only trouble.

In the course of the water there had been several other risings. Secocoeni had Deepened his conflict with the Boers. Griquas and Pondos had revolted in the South of the coastal belt. An alarming rising had occurred on the eastern frontier of the Free State. It seemed as if native tinder was catching fire everywhere. But so far, the flames had been easy to put out. It would be a graver matter if they spread to Zululand.

The Zulus, too, were restless. The drought had not spared them and they had suffered from cattle-disease as well. Tension was inevitable, and it was deepened by the British annexation of the Transvaal. Hitherto Cetewayo had regarded the Boers as his enemies and the British, impersonated in Shepstone, as, by comparison at least, his friends. But now the Boers had suddenly become British subjects, and the check thus given to his militancy was at once apparent.

On the eve of the annexation, as it happened, he had massed his *impis*, some 30,000 strong, on the Transvaal border; and on the day before hoisting the British flag at Pretoria, Shepstone had sent him a message bidding him not to cross it. 'The Dutch have tired me out,' he had replied, 'and I intended to fight them once, only once, and to drive them over the Vaal.'

But since his 'father Somtseu' ordered it, he would send his warriors back to their homes. It was the last time he listened to Shepstone; for there was another unpleasant consequence of the annexation. Together with the Republic, it soon appeared, the British had taken over its territorial quarrel on the Zulu frontier. Hitherto Shepstone had backed Cetewayo's claims. Now he told him he had examined the Boer case and found it justified. 'That liar Somsteu,' Cetewayo exclaimed. It was not an unnatural reaction.

In the winter of 1877 and the spring of 1878, when another bad drought began, the Zulu temper stiffened. And Shepstone for his part had now become convinced that war was unavoidable and that the situation in the Transvaal and indeed in all South Africa would not be eased until the war had been fought and won. He wrote to Carnarvon:

> The sooner the root of the evil, which I consider to be the Zulu power and military organisation, is dealt with, the easier our task will be.

But Carnarvon promptly and firmly put his foot down. In view of the gathering difficulties in Asia and Europe, the fighting in Kaffraria was quite enough. 'A native war,' he told Shepstone in January, 1878, *'is just now impossible and you must avoid it.'* (Underlined in the original). And, in Bulwer's opinion at any rate, war was certainly not yet inevitable. For it seemed that the main cause of friction, the rival claims to the 'disputed territories,' might be peaceably removed. In January Cetewayo was persuaded to agree that the boundary between Zululand and the Transvaal should be determined by arbitration in Natal, and in February Bulwer appointed a commission of three, two Natal officials and Colonel Durnford, R.E., who had served for several years in south-east Africa and knew the country well, to examine the facts and make an award.

They met at Rorke's Drift in March, and, confining themselves to the most disputed area, the country round the Blood River, they unanimously reported in July in favour of the Zulu case, mainly on the legal ground that the cessions of land claimed by the Boers had been made by chiefs without the assent of their councils as native custom required. The report was at once submitted to Bulwer and Frere; but, since it was necessary to inform and consult the Transvaal administration, the publication of the arbitral award was delayed until November. The judgment had taken Frere by surprise, for, like Shepstone, he had thought that the Boer claims or most of them were valid. And it put him in a difficulty, since the chief justification for the annexation of the Transvaal had been the support the Boers would gain from it against the Zulus.

On the other hand, a decision that would antagonise the Boers might conciliate the Zulus. It might be expected to counter the bad effect on Cetewayo's mind of Shepstone's change of front. Bulwer had no doubt in the summer of 1878 that a British-Zulu war could be and should be avoided. Not so Frere, he had written home early in June:

> It is quite clear, that the war spirit is abroad. . . . I have no doubt, and never had, that the Zulus mean mischief.

The subjection of Zululand and neighbouring Swaziland to a British protectorate, he wrote at the end of July, will be found 'necessary sooner or later . . . and the longer it is deferred the more troublesome will the operation become.' It was on August 10 that he posted the dispatch in which he urged his minister to recognise British responsibility up to the Portuguese frontiers.

A disturbing incident occurred in July. Two sons of Sirayo, a Zulu chief who lived close to the frontier on the Buffalo, crossed into Natal with some thirty armed followers, carried off two runaway wives of their father from a local police-station, took them over the border, and put them to death; Bulwer at once demanded the surrender of the ringleaders for trial in Natal. But Cetewayo treated the matter as 'the rash act of boys in the zeal of their father's house,' and only offered an apology and a sum of money. That, of course, was by no means satisfactory; but it was scarcely in itself a *casus belli*, and, writing after the event, Bulwer declared that 'the single affair of Sirayo's sons might have been settled, but the situation was deteriorating all round.'

It was deteriorating in Natal for two main reasons. First, public opinion had been stirred by what might almost be described as a missionary campaign against Cetewayo. In the spring of 1878, despairing of their labours under a regime which had so far spared their own lives but not those of some of their unhappy converts, nearly all the missionaries had withdrawn into Natal where the more militant of them made no secret of their hope that the 'godless' despot would, be overthrown and Zululand subjected to a Christian Government.

Colenso stood almost alone in defending Cetewayo with whom he frequently corresponded, declaring that the more horrible stories of his cruelty were false or overdrawn, and pleading that allowance should be made for a savage ruler who was bound to consider his subjects' feelings and had so far shown no unfriendliness towards Natal.

The second influence making against peace came from military circles. The British troops in Kafiraria were now being moved up to Natal; and in professional soldiers' minds a possible war is readily transmuted into an inevitable war. Here was too much talk in the mess of the coming scrap with the Zulus, and it was over-confident talk. Sir Garnet Wolseley himself, the one first-rate British soldier of his time, who had administered Natal for six months in 1875, had quoted an opinion to Carnarvon, without questioning it, that 1,000 men would suffice for the conquest of Zululand.

Nor was it only soldiers, new to the country, who underestimated Zulu war-power. A leading member of the Legislative Council in Natal, who had lived there for thirty years, told Frere that 'with two hundred red-coats you might march from one end of Zululand to the other.'

It is to the credit of the Natal colonists that neither missionaries nor soldiers made them, as a whole, war-minded. They liked the Zulus who worked for them in Natal. They knew nothing at first hand of what happened over the border. Colenso was quick to detect warmongering in others, but on this issue, at any rate, he championed the colonists. He wrote to a friend in England at the end of 1879:

> Speaking of them generally, I have no hesitation in saying that they never desired the war in the first instance. They never urged it on, or even dreamt of it, till Sir B. Frere came up here and wheedled them into following his lead and supporting him in his undertaking to relieve them from the "standing menace" of the Zulu power.

And then this characteristically candid admission:

> For, of course the Zulu military system was in some sense a "standing menace" to the peace of Natal, and some accidental circumstance, either under Cetewayo or under some other king, might have brought the Zulu Army over our borders.

That danger had haunted colonial homes lor some years past. Dingaan's raid to the sea was not so long ago and it had not been forgotten. But fear of a Zulu invasion cut both ways. It made men want a war to break the Zulu power; but it also made them anxious as to what might possibly happen when the war began. The long frontier was virtually left unguarded. And might not the thousands of Zulus within it rise and join their kinsfolk?

For lack of evidence, it is less easy to determine what was passing in Cetewayo's mind. Certainly, the annexation of the Transvaal and Shepstone's betrayal, as he regarded it, made him more truculent. The tone of his letter about Sirayo's sons was far from conciliatory, still less submissive. Two months after that incident, moreover, Mbeline, a Swazi chief resident in Zululand, raided the native *kraals* within the Transvaal border; and Mbeline was known as Cetewayo's 'dog' who did what his master told him. A *kraal*, too, was built in the 'disputed territory': it was for an *induna*, it was said, who would rule the natives there. But it was to be hoped that the boundary award—the terms of which were known at that time (September) to the British authorities—might put an end to friction on that frontier.

In any case, since Secocoeni's triumph and the annexation, the Boers had abstained from provoking Zulu hostility. It was British conduct during those critical months that seemed to Cetewayo—so he said—to be provocative. British reinforcements were arriving. Five companies of the 1/24th Foot, (the Warwickshires, now the South Wales Borderers), released from the 'Kaffir War,' marched up into Natal. Other troops arrived by sea from Mauritius and from England. What were they all for? A small column occupied Utrecht Two companies garrisoned Luneburg. These townships were in the 'disputed' area, where troops were possibly needed to ensure that the imminent demarcation of the frontier was now respected.

But they were also *points d'appui* for an invasion of Zululand. Bulwer, indeed, said afterwards that Zulu uneasiness had been sharply enhanced by these troop movements, and he complained of their unwisdom at the time so firmly and repeatedly as to strain even Frere's unfailing patience. But, granted the provocation, was it sufficient to spur Cetewayo into liking the offensive? To one who weighs the conflicting opinions of that time and the character of those who held them it seems probable that Cetewayo had made up his mind to fight rather than submit to any serious interference in the domestic affairs of Zululand, but that, while there were limits, no doubt, to his power to hold his 'celibate man-destroying gladiators' (as Frere called them) in leash, he did not mean to be the first to break the peace if he could help it.

5

Such was the situation, such the atmosphere, when Frere, who had been detained in the south by the post-war settlement, came up to Pietermaritzburg (September 28). The reports he had received at Capetown had already convinced him that the danger of a concerted native rebellion was real and that all the threads of it ran back to Cetewayo. Shepstone had written:

There is at this moment, a process of political fermentation going on among all the native tribes from the colonial sea-board to the Zambesi.

And where, asked Frere, was this restlessness most acute? 'Wherever,' he answered, 'the Zulu influence is felt.' And again, he begged for reinforcements from home. His first impressions at Pietermaritzburg more than confirmed his diagnosis. The position, he declared in a dispatch to the Secretary of State written two days after his arrival, was 'far more critical even than I expected.' He added in a covering letter:

'The people here seem slumbering on a volcano. I much fear you will not be able to send out the reinforcements we have asked for in time to prevent an explosion. . . . The Zulus are now quite out of hand, and the maintenance of peace depends on their forbearance. . . . I speak with a deep sense of responsibility for what I say when I assure you that the peace of South Africa for many years to come seems to me to depend on your taking steps to put a final end to Zulu pretensions.'

Frere was engaged in discussing the military plans for the war he now thought to be imminent when on November 4, he was startled and dismayed by a cable from the Colonial Office refusing reinforcements. In due course an explanatory dispatch informed him that the Cabinet believed that:

By the exercise of prudence and by meeting the Zulus in a spirit of forbearance and reasonable compromise, it will be possible to avert the very serious evil of a war with Cetewayo.

It seemed to Frere that all his arguments, all his warnings, had been completely ignored in London; and he was entitled to resent the fact that this refusal of reinforcements was the first intimation he had received that his masters in Whitehall were not in full agreement with his policy. He realised, no doubt, that the resignation of Carnarvon on an issue of foreign policy at the beginning of the year might have weakened his own authority. Hicks Beach, who had succeeded Carnarvon, had far less interest in South Africa and far less knowledge of its problems. Federation, moreover, had always been regarded by his colleagues as Carnarvon's personal affair—he had himself described it as 'my Confederation policy'—and his successor was not so deeply committed to support the man Carnarvon had chosen to carry it out.

But Frere had re-drawn in his dispatches to Hicks Beach the main lines of his policy; and Hicks Beach's dispatches to him, though less full and frequent than Carnarvon's, had been no less sympathetic. The gist of them had been as follows:

April 4: Zulu raids on the 'disputed territory' must be stopped.

July 11: When the boundary has been fixed by arbitration, it 'must be upheld at whatever cost.'

July 25: 'I see the troops are being very properly moved to that part of the country, so that they will be ready if necessary to enforce the observance of your award.'

Then, after the summer holiday, October 2: 'Of course, Cetewayo must be kept in order, and compelled to give up Zulus who violate Natal or Transvaal territory.'

Three days later the tone began to change. October 5: 'There should still be a good chance of avoiding war with the Zulus.'

October 10: 'I hope a Zulu war may not be necessary.'

Up to this time, it is evident, Hicks Beach and his advisers at the Colonial Office had been in two minds. They did not want a war—not yet, at any rate—owing to the increasing international tension in Europe and Asia; but they hesitated to question the judgment, so confidently and lucidly expressed, of a man of Frere's great reputation. It was only the imminence of war with Afghanistan—it began on November 21—and the belief that war with Russia might soon follow that settled the balance at last and firmly against yet another war in Zululand.

Hence the refusal of reinforcements after critical discussion in the Cabinet. Hence the plain language now used for the first time by Hicks Beach about the possibility of averting 'the very serious evil' of a war. Even so, it was not till November 7, on receipt of Frere's first dispatch from Pietermaritzburg, that the war was positively forbidden as Carnarvon had forbidden it ten months earlier. Hicks Beach wrote:

> *We cannot now have a Zulu war, in addition to other greater and too possible troubles.* (Underlined in the original).

On November 20, however, hearing that Frere's request was firmly backed by General Thesiger commanding in Natal and by Bulwer, the Cabinet reluctantly conceded it; but Frere was told that the reinforcements were solely for the defence of Natal. Hicks Beach had complained a fortnight earlier:

> I really cannot control him without a telegraph, I don't know that I could with one. I feel it is as likely as not that he is at war with the Zulus at the present moment.

★★★★★★★★★★

At this the cable had not been laid beyond St Vincent, one of the Cape Verde Islands, whence telegram were taken by ship to Capetown, and on by overland telegraph to Natal. The quickest telegram on record at this period was the one in which Frere reported the news of Isandhlwana. It left Pietermaritzburg on January 27, caught the mailboat leaving Capetown next day, and was delivered at the Colonial Office at 13.30 a.m. on February 12. Letters, of course took much longer. Dispatches from Capetown usually took 22 days to reach London, from. Pietermaritzburg 33 and often more.

★★★★★★★★★★

And, though Hicks Beach had made no attempt to control him earlier—despite his clear intimations as to where his policy was leading—it was true enough that by the middle of October he could no longer be controlled. Rightly or wrongly, he had made up his mind that the situation had become so dangerous that he could not retreat. To the first refusal of reinforcements, he replied with a powerful restatement of his case (November 5). He wrote:

> There can be no doubt, that a feeling of extreme self-confidence and anxiety to try conclusions with the white man pervades the whole mass of Zulus.

The annexation of the Transvaal has made them anti-British and the Boers are so disgruntled by it that they are not unlikely to hold aloof in the event of war. Nor can we expect the Boers to acquiesce in our rule if we do not afford them that protection from the Zulu danger which is its main justification. It would be wrong to coerce the Zulus in order to secure the allegiance of the Transvaal if the Zulus could be persuaded to remain within their borders. But that is impossible, and the effect of our toleration of Zulu power goes far beyond the Transvaal. From the Fish River to the Limpopo and from the Orange to Delagoa Bay 'the influence of the Zulu king has been found at work.'

Nor was it only a sudden and concerted outbreak that Frere dreaded. He also believed that at any moment the intransigent section of the Boers might raise a rebellion in the Transvaal. If that should happen, nothing could prevent Cetewayo's warriors from joining in the fight—and almost certainly on the British side. What then? Would not a wave of anti-British race-feeling run through all Dutch South Africa from the Vaal to the Cape? So critical, in fact, was the whole situation that the gathering clouds in Asia and Europe were not an argument in Frere's view for postponing a settlement with the Zulus. On the contrary, they made a compelling case for hastening it on, so that the peace of South Africa could be secured before the storm broke elsewhere.

With such dark thoughts in his mind, it is plain that, well before Hicks Beach penned his veto on November 5, Frere had decided to bring the issue quickly to a head; and, whether or not he expected his eleventh-hour arguments to convince the Cabinet, he went quietly on with his plans for 'putting a final end' to Zulu militarism. The veto reached him on December 13.

Two days earlier he had delivered his ultimatum to Cetewayo's envoys on the frontier.

★★★★★★★★★★

In Lady Victoria Hicks Beach's biography of her father (London, 1933) it is stated that Lady Frere telegraphed a summary of the letter of November 7 from Cape Town and that this summary reached Frere at Pietermaritzburg on November 30. Since the text of it had apparently been lost, it is impossible to say to what extent, if at all, it made the veto clear.

★★★★★★★★★★

The occasion of the ultimatum was the announcement of the boundary award. Frere thought the award was unjust to the Boers, but he did not feel entitled to vary it: he could only make it a condition of its execution that the Boers settled in the territory ceded to the Zulus should be compensated if they chose to go or protected if they chose to stay. It was partly, no doubt, to weaken the effect of it, both in the Transvaal and in Zululand, but mainly, it seems certain, because of the opportunity it gave him of forcing the issue that Frere coupled the award with a series of demands that had nothing directly to do with it.

The three ringleaders in the abduction of Sirayo's wives were to be surrendered within twenty days to stand their trial in Natal, together with a fine of 500 cattle for the failure to comply with the earlier request. A smaller fine was imposed for interfering with a British surveying party on the Natal side of the border. Mbeline was also to be handed over.

These minor demands were humiliating enough, but what followed was far more serious. The undertakings given at Cetewayo's coronation to prohibit indiscriminate killing were henceforth to be observed. The Zulu military system was to be drastically reformed—in particular all men must be allowed to marry when of age—and, while the general obligation to serve in war might be retained, the army was not to be mobilised without the consent not only of the Great Council but also of the British Government. Missionaries and their converts were to be protected as in Panda's time. Finally, to see that these conditions were kept, a British Resident would be appointed to deal direct with King and Council on the British Governor's behalf. For the acceptance of these demands ten more days were allowed.

If, as Colenso had strongly maintained, Cetewayo wanted peace, he might well have submitted to all of those demands save one; but to that one, as Frere must have known, he could not submit. The Zulu Army, as has been seen, was the Zulu nation. For Cetewayo to surrender the ultimate control of it to the Council and the British Government was at one stroke to destroy the basis of his own kingly power and the independence of his country. No: the challenge might be welcome or unwelcome, but in any case, he could not yield to it. The military clauses of the ultimatum were virtually a declaration of war. The twenty days went by and no answer came from Cetewayo. Ten more days, and still silence. On the thirty-first day the British troops crossed the frontier into Zululand.

It was Frere's war, but the blame he incurred for it in England was, as will be seen later on, a good deal more than he deserved. No one denied, not Colenso himself, that Zulu militarism was a 'standing menace.' That the peace of South Africa required its removal sooner or later, and by force if nothing else availed, was no less undeniable. But was Frere justified in discarding diplomacy and using force with so little delay? The answer to that depends on facts which can never be established. Frere's temper was not *bellicose*: his whole career in India was proof of that. Nor was he liable to panic: he had shown quite remarkable coolness in the worst days of the Mutiny. But he evidently believed not only that the 'black peril' was real but also that it was imminent.

At any moment, he seems to have thought, the storm might break. And even if there was insufficient evidence for the existence of a great Bantu conspiracy to drive the white men into the sea, there was danger enough in Zululand alone and its proximity to the long and ill-defended frontier of Natal. If a Zulu invasion was coming, the only way to stop it, he believed, was to forestall it by a British invasion. Otherwise, the Zulus could choose their time and place and sweep across the Colony. It was that danger and no more that troubled the sober Bulwer. He did not think that war had always been unavoidable, but, owing to the worsening of the atmosphere, he did think it could not be avoided in the autumn of 1878, And, that being so, there seemed, he said afterwards, 'to be nothing left but to grasp the nettle firmly.' So he added his signature to the ultimatum.

There was another question. Sir Henry Taylor, who had served in the Colonial Office, wrote:

> Frere may have been right in the conception that a conflict with Cetewayo was inevitable but he was wrong in taking it upon himself to provoke one. . . . I think he has lost his sense of subordination.

But Frere's post was not an, ordinary governorship—he would not have accepted one—he was also High-Commissioner and Governor-General designate. His position was comparable with his membership of the Government of India which enjoyed a higher status than that of a Colonial Government and which was allowed in those days to go on its way without much interference by the India Office. He had been sent out by Carnarvon 'to carry out his scheme,' and he was probably right if he supposed that Carnarvon intended him to have a pretty free hand; but, with a due 'sense of subordination,' he had told his chief what the execution of his policy implied.

> The trial of strength will be forced on you, and neither justice nor humanity will be served by postponing the trial if we start with a good cause.

He had repeated this warning to Hicks Beach in the summer of 1878. 'You must be master up to the Portuguese frontier.' And not one hint had reached him that the Secretary of State or any of his colleagues disagreed. Yet, if Frere could claim that a conflict with the Zulus was implicit in all he had said, it seems fair to say that he ought to have made it more explicit. If Hicks Beach was to blame for not asking for concrete information as to his plans, was not Frere equally to blame for not furnishing it unasked? Should he not have told Hicks Beach not only that he expected the war quite soon, but that he intended to force the issue at the earliest opportunity? Should he not have communicated the terms of his ultimatum in time for the Cabinet to comment on them? As it was, he did not dispatch the text till five days after it had been delivered and it did not arrive in London till January 2, nine days before the war began. That Frere, lastly, could not obey the veto on war when it reached him seems indisputable. It was too late. To have delivered the ultimatum and, if it were not accepted, to do nothing but stand on the defensive was surely quite impossible.

In the last resort it was a question of the amount of individual responsibility that should be conceded to an agent of the British Government operating thousands of miles away from London and debarred from quick communication with his superiors. Frere's experience was in favour of giving plenty of rope to 'the man on the spot.' It was a tradition in India that British officials, from a district officer upwards, should take grave decisions at need on their own responsibility. If the outcome was bad, their action was not too severely reprimanded. If it was good, it was not only confirmed but applauded. And in this case Frere confidently expected the latter result. He believed the Zulus would be conquered in a brief campaign at little cost of life and money.

Impressed by this exhibition of military strength, the recalcitrant Boers would acquiesce in British sovereignty over the Transvaal. And then the reunion of South Africa under a single paramount power from the Cape to the Portuguese frontiers would be only a matter of time. But the first step must be swift and firm. The Zulu war, he had written, must begin and end with 'a sharp and decisive success.' *Dis aliter visum*.

VIEWS OF ISANDLWANA

Isandhlwana

1

For the coming tragedy at Isandhlwana two men, because of the positions they held in the field, were, formally at any rate, more responsible than anyone else. One was the Commander-in-Chief, the other a Colonel of the Royal Engineers.

Frederic Augustus Thesiger was born in 1827, the eldest son of the first Lord Chelmsford, Lord Chancellor in the second and third Derby ministries. He joined the Grenadier Guards at the age of seventeen, and, ten years later, served with distinction in the Crimean War, He was on Napier's staff in the Abyssinian War in 1868, and became adjutant-general in India in 1869. From 1874 onwards he held commands in England. He was promoted major-general in 1877, and in 1878 he obtained the local rank of lieutenant-general on his appointment to succeed Sir Arthur Cunynghame in command of the British forces in South Africa.

His record so far was proof that he possessed considerable ad-ministrative gifts; but it was an almost wholly peace-time record, and the efficient conduct of manoeuvres was scarcely better evidence than youthful service in the Crimea or staff-work on the road to Magdala of ability to command an army in the field. But if the quality of his generalship had yet to be established, there had never been any doubts about the merits of his character and personality. He was as incapable of insincerity or intrigue as he was of discourtesy. He always spoke in the warmest terms of the officers and men he commanded and insisted that their services should be recognised as they deserved.

LORD CHELMSFORD

And, unlike some more successful soldiers of his age, he was a modest man, too modest it was thought by those who complained of his readiness to change his mind in deference to other opinions. Such men are likeable, and everyone who had to do with Thesiger—or Chelmsford as he became at his father's death in October, 1878—everyone from the High Commissioner to the private soldier liked him and respected him.

One other virtue must be recorded. Good soldiers are never inhumane, and, if Chelmsford meant to fight hard, he meant to fight cleanly. On the eve of his advance, he made it clear that his native troops must observe the rules of war, however their enemies might break them. Anyone killing a woman or a child or a wounded man might be hanged. Anyone, white or black, setting fire to a hut without specific authority from his column commander might be flogged.

On, his arrival in South Africa, the new C. in C. found the British forces already engaged in suppressing the Gaika and Galeka rebellion, and in less than four months he was able to report to the War Office that the fighting was over, that the rebel chiefs Sandile, was dead, and that an amnesty had been proclaimed and peace concluded, In his report to his superiors in London he gave the main credit for this success to his British regular troops—which included the first and second battalions of the 34th Foot—but the War Office was sufficiently impressed with his own conduct of the operations to recommend the award of a K.C.B. At the end of the war, he went to stay with Frere at Capetown, and there, not unnaturally, he was soon convinced that he would have to take the field again before very long. He wrote home in July:

> It is more than probable, that active steps will have to be taken to check the arrogance of Cetewayo.

Those steps, he realised, must be substantial and well-prepared. He wrote to Shepstone in the summer of 1878:

> If we are to have a fight with the Zulus, I am anxious that our arrangements should be as complete as it is possible

to make them. Half measures do not answer with natives. They must be thoroughly crushed to make them believe in our superiority; and, if I am called upon to conduct operations against them, I shall strive to be in a position to show them how hopelessly inferior they are to us in fighting power although numerically stronger.

That did not mean, as was subsequently charged against him, that Chelmsford absurdly underestimated the difficulties and dangers of a Zulu war. He was well aware that Cetewayo's massed regiments were far more formidable than Sandile's handful of ill-disciplined tribesmen; and, though he was prepared to take the offensive with the troops at his disposal, he strongly supported, as has been seen, Frere's request for reinforcements. In November he asked for two more battalions to be sent out as soon as possible. They were needed, he argued, for defence alone against possible Zulu raids over the Natal and Transvaal frontiers, a stretch of some 200 miles with no lateral communications. They would be still more needed if Zululand were to be invaded. In conducting operations against an enemy like the Kaffir or the Zulu, *the first blow struck should be a heavy one*, (author's italics), and I am satisfied that no greater mistake can be made than to attempt to conquer him with insufficient means.'

As proof of his urgent need of 'extra assistance,' he had asked for any such naval force as could be spared. The seamen were on the spot and made available without delay. A naval brigade of 170 sailors and marines with some light artillery disembarked from H.M.S. *Active* and *Tenedos* on November 19. For the reasons stated above, the military reinforcements were not provided so quickly. The two battalions he had asked for did not reach Durban till January, 1879.

Chelmsford's plan of invasion, if invasion it was to be, was simple. His objective was the occupation of Ulundi, Cetewayo's capital, which lay about fifty-five miles due east of the Natal frontier on the River Buffalo at Rorke's Drift. No insurmountable obstacles barred his path. Most of Zululand is a country of rolling downs. Save for a belt of forest near the Tugela, the land

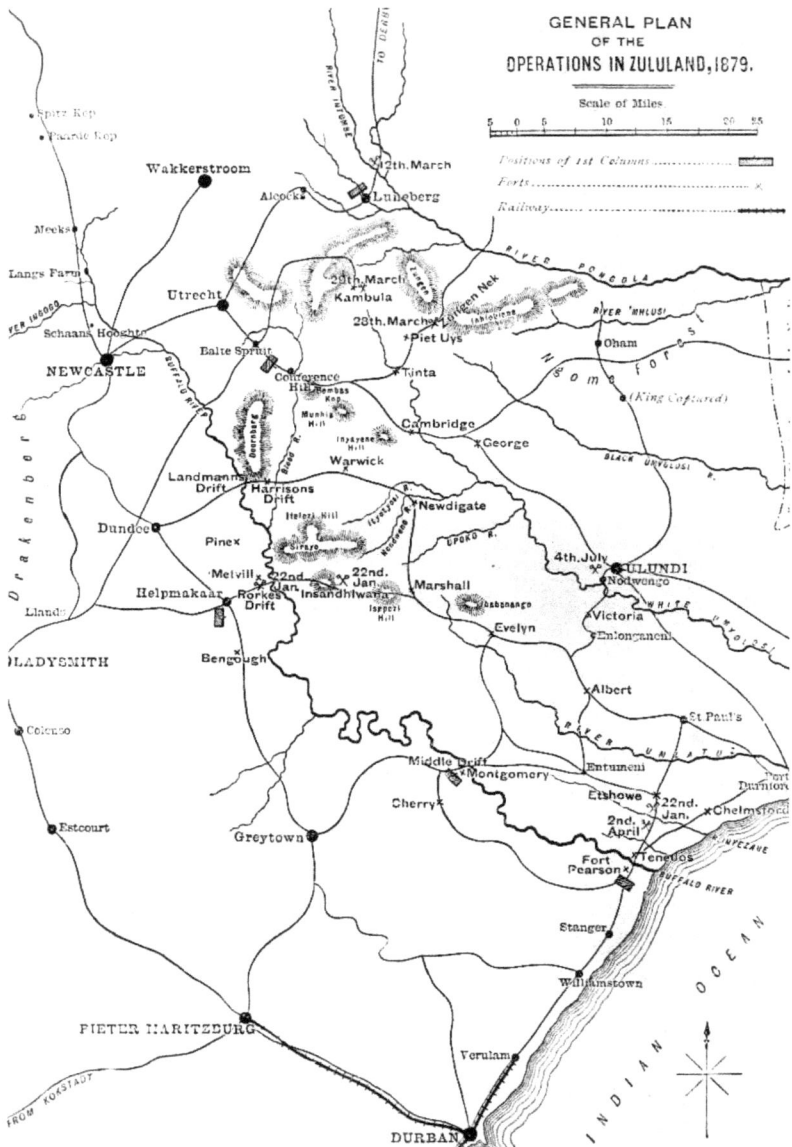

GENERAL PLAN OF THE OPERATIONS IN ZULULAND, 1879.

is almost bare of trees, but it is studded with those outcrops of sandstone, rising sometimes to mountain height, which strike the stranger as the most remarkable feature of the South African landscape at any distance from the coast. No broad river crosses this area, only gullies or *dongas* cut by streams with little, if any, water in them for most of the year. The terrain, in fact, presented only one serious difficulty to a white invading army: there were no roads, and the native tracks might be quickly rendered impassable for wagons by the heavy thunderstorms to be expected in the early months of the year. This was a one-sided handicap. The Zulus, as has been pointed out, could move over almost any ground, and three times as fast—Chelmsford himself remarked—as a column of British infantry.

Because of this lack of roads Chelmsford expected his advance to be slow. But he meant it to be sure. He discarded the idea of concentrating his forces for a single massive drive at Ulundi. No doubt he could have got through, but it would have made it possible for the Zulus on either flank to creep round towards his rear and threaten his communications or to invade Natal. He told Frere:

> The plan I have laid down, is not so ambitious a one as a rapid march upon Ulundi and the occupation of the king's *kraal*, but I am certain it is the only safe one under the circumstances. It would be impossible to keep a long line of road passable for a convoy of wagons, and were we to advance far into the country it would be almost certain that, instead of our supplies coming to us, we should have to return for our supplies A retrograde movement would have a very bad effect on our native forces and would certainty encourage our enemies.

His plan was to advance in three columns along separate routes converging on Ulundi. The frontier would thus be secured, and the Zulus pushed steadily away from it. If they evaded action and fell back to protect Ulundi, all the better. He converging columns would unite to confront the united Zulu

Army and thus be able, it might be hoped, to win such, a crushing victory as to end the war outright. Strategists will probably agree that this was a good plan and, given good timing, likely to achieve its object.

On the morrow of the ultimatum the British forces were taking up position in accordance with this plan. The Right Column under Colonel Pearson was stationed near the mouth of the Tugela with orders, if war came, to cross the river and move north and occupy the mission station at Eshowe. It was composed of the 2/3rd Foot and six companies of the 99th, one company R.E., the Naval Brigade, several squadrons of mounted infantry, mostly colonial, and the second regiment of the Natal Native Contingent (N.N.C.) with two R.A. seven-pounders, one Gatling and two rocket tubes. The total strength was 4,750, of which about 1,900 were white men.

The Left Column under Colonel Wood was based on Utrecht with orders to cross the Blood River and advance southeast to Inyayeni Hill. It consisted of the 1/13th Foot, the 90th Foot, some 200 colonial fight horse, 380 N.N.C. with six R.A. seven-pounders and two rockets, and a small volunteer commando of mounted Boers from the Utrecht district, led by the veteran Piet Uys. Total strength 2,278; white men about 1,800. The Central Column under Colonel Glyn was to start across the Buffalo from Rorke's Drift and march due east. It consisted of the 1/24th and 2/24th Foot, five squadrons of colonial mounted infantry and police, one company R.E., the third regiment of the N.N.C. with six R.A. seven-pounders and two rockets. Total strength, 4,709: white men about 1,750.

A fourth column under Colonel Durnford was held in reserve to protect the frontier at the outset and then to advance between the right and central columns through the belt of forest which lay between the Tugela valley and the bare uplands of central Zululand. Its base was on the Tugela at Kranz Kop, near the river crossing known as Middle Drift, it was composed entirely of native troops—the three battalions of the first N.N.C. regiment, a squadron of native cavalry, mostly Basutos, and a

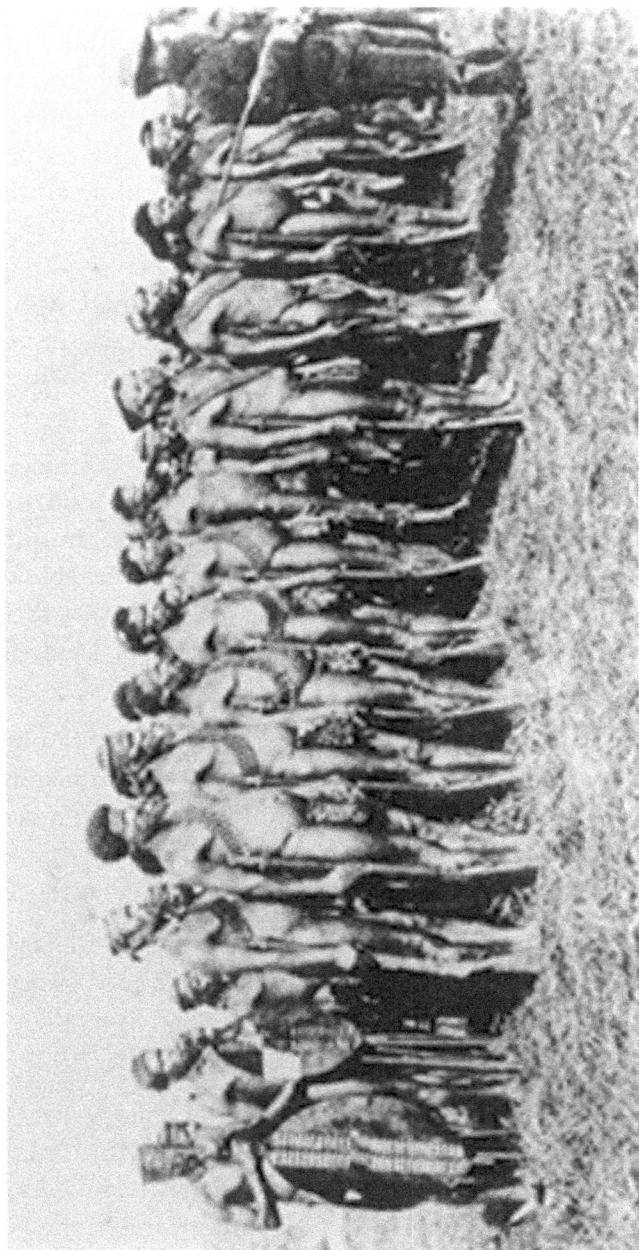

Natal Native Contingent

company of native pioneers. Total strength, 3,871.

Chelmsford had decided to accompany the Central Column, and on January 10, the date, on which the ultimatum expired, he moved his headquarters to Rorke's Drift. It was now virtually certain that war would begin next day, but it was still hoped that at an early stage of the invasion Cetewayo, seeing that the British were in deadly earnest, would realise the hopelessness of resistance and submit.

In any case Chelmsford was confident of his capacity to carry out the task entrusted to him. Nor had he any doubts as to the wisdom of that forward policy of which his army was to be the spearpoint. He wholly agreed with Frere, he wrote to him on January 11:

> I trust, that before long the troops under my command may have an opportunity of settling, once and for all, the Zulu question. . . . Our cause will be a good one. In spite of all the Colenso party may say, and I hope to be able to convince them all before many weeks are over that for a savage, as for a child, timely severity is greater kindness than mistaken leniency. . .

But by 'many weeks' he meant what he said. Writing on January 8 to the Duke of Cambridge, he said that Zululand was rumoured to be 'in a state of utter confusion' and no one could guess what the Zulu tactics would be. But, in any event the weather and the state of the roads ruled out a rapid advance.

> If I wished to make a rush, I should be unable to carry it out. . . . Our movements will all be made in the most deliberate manner.

2

The other protagonist in the impending tragedy was Anthony William Durnford, eldest son of General Durnford, R.E. Born on his father's estate in Co. Leitrim in 1830 and educated in Ireland and Germany, he obtained a commission in the Royal Engineers in 1848; and, after serving in Ceylon and in other oversea posts, and at Devonport, he was ordered to the Cape in 1872. (When he was desperately ill with heat apoplexy in Ceylon in 1865, his life was saved by the devoted nursing of 'Chinese Gordon.') In 1873 he was attached to the official delegation which attended the coronation of Cetewayo. He wrote in one of the long, lively letters he sent by nearly every mail to his mother in Ireland:

> The Zulus are a warlike race, every man a soldier and ever armed. . . . At the coronation of the king about 5,000 of his warriors were present, and a wild lot they looked. They sang a war song—a song without words, wonderfully impressive as the waves of sound rose, fell and died away, then rose again in a mournful strain, yet warlike in the extreme.

Later in that year, Durnford served as chief of staff with the mixed force of British troops and Basutos on their expedition against Langalibalele. At the outset of the operations, he was ordered to occupy Bushman's River Pass with a small force, and at the end of an exhausting march he found himself confronted with a considerable body of hostile natives. He could probably have dispersed them by a vigorous attack, but he was under strict orders not to fire the first shot, and the failure of some young untried colonial volunteers to stand the strain led to a disorderly retreat.

Three of the volunteers were killed. Durnford himself had a miraculous escape. His shoulder had been dislocated by a fall on the march up, and he was wounded in the same arm by an *assegai*. But he fought his way back with a courage for which, in the opinion of two members of the subsequent court of enquiry, he deserved the V.C. Men might question his opinions, but none his bravery. Colonel Pearson of the Right Column wrote after his death:

> He was a fine chivalrous soldier, and a man of admirable personal courage.

None the less, he was unpopular among the colonists of Natal. To begin with, they blamed him, quite unfairly, for the death of those volunteers; and, when he had lived that down, they were alienated by his outspoken championship of native rights, particularly with regard to the injustice done to Langalibalele's tribesmen. They disapproved, moreover, of his personal relations with the natives. For Durnford, like many others of his kind, felt a spontaneous liking for the African native. 'Fine men,' was his first immediate impression, 'very naked and all that sort of thing, but thoroughly good fellows.' And, if the natives in service of one sort or another in Pietermaritzburg were somewhat more sophisticated, they had, he thought, redeeming virtues.

> The streets of this city, as large as a village in England, are full of savages from morn to night, and a jollier lot I never saw, ever laughing, singing and dancing. Send a "boy" (they are all "boys") on a message, he dances down the street; look, even, at him, he grins from ear to ear.

Most of the colonists shared this liking; but it was not so easy for them to share Durnford's sense of human equality with these backward folk, and they resented his treating them as equals. It was a natural difference. Durnford, after all, was spending only a few years of his life in Natal. The colonists, with their wives and children, had made their ill-protected homes there, for good and all, with that vast black barbarous multitude at their very doors.

So Durnford was a rather lonely figure in Natal society, but he was not quite alone. The more sober-minded colonists agreed with him that relations between the races should be founded on strict British justice. So did the editor of at least one local newspaper, the *Natal Colonist*. Above all, his 'negrophilism' won him the close friendship of the arch-negrophilist, Colenso. He wrote soon after their first meeting:

> The bishop is a man of men, he would go to his death for the right.

He became a frequent guest at Colenso's house at Pietermaritzburg, and before long he had come to regard him as 'the man

I respect and, reverence most in the world.' The attraction was mutual. Colenso's biographer records that his acquaintance with Durnford 'rapidly ripened into the most intimate friendship of his later life.' Another Englishman who recognised Durnford's high qualities was Froude who came across him in the course of his second visit to South Africa, he told Colenso:

> I have rarely met a man, who at first sight made a more pleasing impression upon me. He was more than I expected, and his distinguished reputation had led me to form very high expectations indeed.

Except on the point of courage, these good opinions were not shared in higher military circles. The soldiers, like most of, the colonists, disapproved of Durnford's interference in native affairs. It was a matter of principle. A soldier should have no 'politics.' He should never question government decisions. Such an attitude was not unnatural, and it probably accounted for Durnford's transfer, to another post. In 1876, after some years' service as head of the Engineer's Department in Natal, he was sent to Mauritius, where, on medical advice, he obtained permission to go home for treatment. But, early in 1877, he was called back to Natal. The position was becoming critical. The storm clouds were banking up over Zululand, and all the tribes on the colonial borders were in a state of dangerous tension.

In such a situation the value of Durnford, however awkward his 'politics' might be, was unquestionable. He understood the natives far better than any other soldier, and the Langalibalele campaign had shown that he exercised over them in the field an effortless authority. The Basutos, for example, under his command—and there were no more useful native auxiliaries than those bold hillsmen on their wiry ponies—had shown a trust in him and a personal devotion not often accorded to a British officer. So Durnford was brought back, and, as the horizon darkened, he was allotted two important tasks. In February, 1878, he was appointed to the Boundary Commission. In the following autumn, promoted previously to a brevet-colonelcy, he was or-

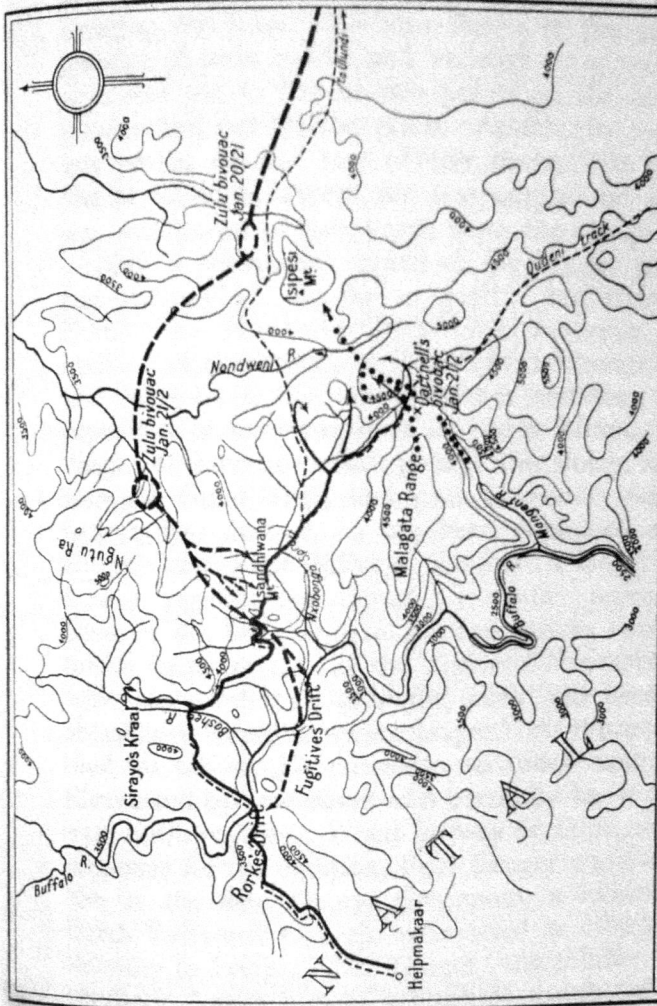

The Campaign of Isandhlwana Jan. 12-22, 1879

Lord Chelmsford's march to Isandhlwana and the movements of his field force on the 22nd. Zulu movements in black : ———▶ advance of the main impi; ••••▶ tribal force attacked by the British; Contours at 500 ft. intervals : heights above sea-level SCALE OF MILES

Figure 1

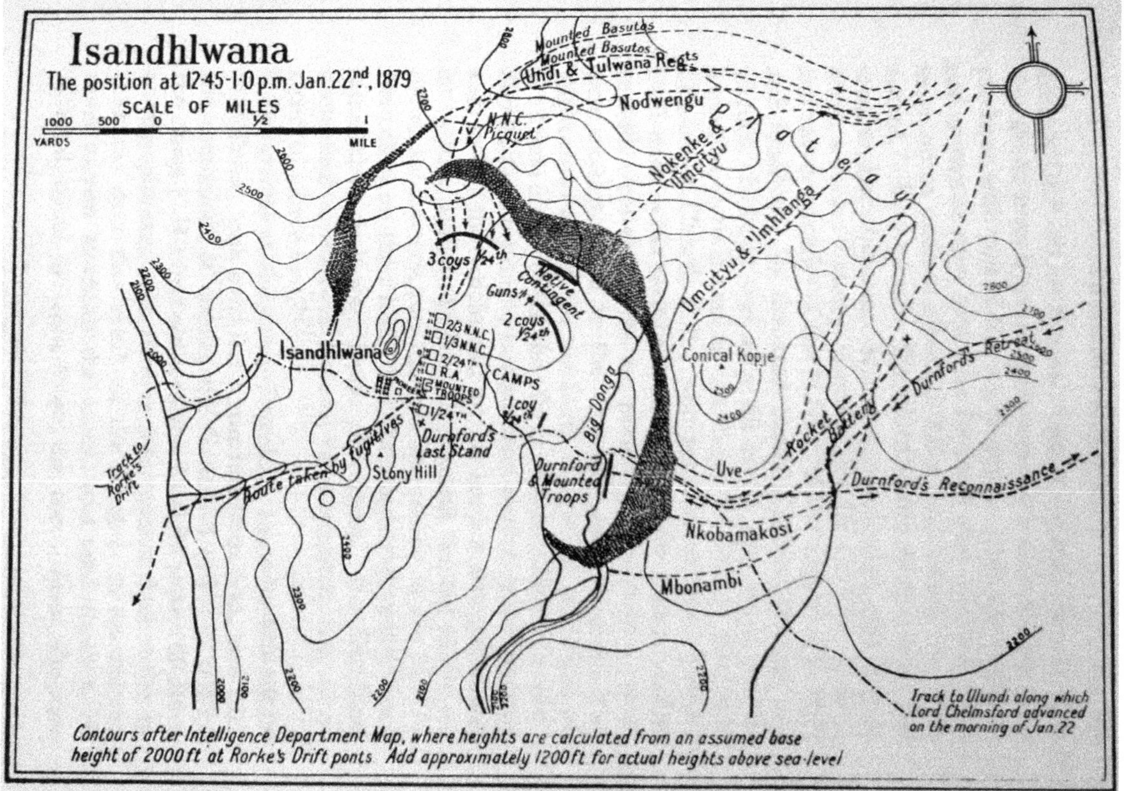

Isandhlwana

The position at 12·45-1·0 p.m. Jan. 22nd, 1879

SCALE OF MILES

1000 500 0 ½ 1 MILE
YARDS

Mounted Basutos
Mounted Basutos
24th & Ulwana Regts
Nodwengu

Nokenke & Nodwengu
Umcityu & Imihlanga

Conical Kopje

Rocket Ravine

Durnford's Retreat

Durnford's Reconnaissance

Uve
Nkobamakosi
Mbonambi

Big Donga

Durnford & Mounted Troops

Native Contingent
Guns 2 coys
3 coys
2 coys
CAMPS
20 N.N.C.
2/24th
1/3 N.N.C.
R.A.
1/24th
Mounted Troops
Fugitives
Durnford's Last Stand
Stony Hill
Route taken by Fugitives
Route taken by Fugitives

Isandhlwana

Contours after Intelligence Department Map, where heights are calculated from an assumed base
height of 2000 ft, Add approximately 1200 ft for actual heights above sea-level
(200 ft at Rorke's Drift ponts.

Track to Ulundi along which
Lord Chelmsford advanced
on the morning of Jan 22

Figure 2

dered to raise the Natal Native Contingent, part of which, as has been recorded, was put under his command to form the reserve column. But, almost to the last moment, he could not bring himself to believe that war was inevitable.

He did not minimise the danger of Zulu hostility. He took a for more serious view of it than Colenso. He had repeatedly pointed out that Natal was very ill-protected against the possibility of a sudden Zulu attack. The Zulus, he once remarked, could 'rush' Pietermaritzburg from the frontier within twenty-four hours. Nor was he a sentimentalist. He wrote in 1875:

> Not that I would be too tender with the savage. No: but I would be just to him, just to the last degree.

He held that a just settlement of the boundary dispute should be made and firmly maintained. If the Zulus refused to accept it, they must be compelled to do so by threat of war, by war itself in the last resort by the subjection of Zululand to British rule. It may be said, in fact, that Durnford's Zulu policy was much the same as Frere's. But there was this crucial difference. Frere believed that the Zulus would not be satisfied by any settlement, that they meant sooner or later to fight, that war and annexation were unavoidable. Those were not Durnford's beliefs. Till the eleventh hour he clung stubbornly to his conviction that there would be no war. He had written early in 1878:

> Cetewayo is anxious for a peaceful settlement of the boundary, the Zulus don't want to fight at all and peace will be maintained.

The Commission's award confirmed his optimism, Even the arrival of an officer of general's rank did not shake it, he wrote in August:

> General here, just sent for. He . . . has cooled down from the war fever considerably since he has been under the governor's influence.

Again, as late as November, when he is already raising the N.N.C.:

I like the general much. He is a *gentleman*, and that says everything. Peace still prevails here, and may yet do so for many years to come. The Zulus are not at all inclined to fight, and have nothing to fight for as yet.

When, a few weeks later, the ultimatum came, he realised what it meant. He put his 'politics' aside. Almost certainly now it was to be a soldier's affair, and he would do his soldier's duty.

So, the new year found him, in command of his native column, facing Zululand across the Tugela at Kranz Kop. There he remained for a fortnight, busily training his men. His health was good and his spirits high. He had written a little earlier:

I have my hands full of work, but like it above everything. . . Were the weather not so wet the life would be most enjoyable, but damp *is* a " damper." . . . I wonder whether you would admire my appearance for the field? Boots, spurs, dark cord-breeches, serge patrol-jacket, broad belt over the shoulders and one round the waist—to the former a revolver and to the latter a hunting knife and ammunition pouch. A wideawake soft felt hat with wide brim, one side turned up, and a crimson turban wound round the hat— very like a stage brigand!

Chelmsford had decided, as has been said, that Durnford's column should not take part in the invasion abreast of the other columns but should act in support of the Central Column. Durnford, therefore, was directed to wait at Kranz Kop for orders, but he had not yet received them when, in the second week of January, information reached him—in the light of subsequent events it was probably untrue—from a missionary still resident in Zululand that the Zulus were gathering northwards of Kranz Kop for an invasion of Natal.

Durnford determined on his own initiative to order a reconnaissance in force, and, in the early hours of January 14, having sent a rider to report his movement to Chelmsford at Rorke's Drift, he set his column on the march towards the river. The troops were naturally elated at the move.

'We are in for a lark at last,' said one of his officers: 'the colonel means going for Cetewayo, and we shall be into Ulundi before the general yet.'

But, before they reached the river-crossing, an orderly galloped up with a note from Chelmsford. As it happened, the time had come for Durnford's column to take position in rear of the centre, and Chelmsford was taken aback at the news of his unauthorised move. The note was a stiff reprimand. If Durnford acted again independently and without orders, he would be relieved of his command.

'I well remember,' recorded one of his officers, 'the look of disgust which crossed his countenance as he read the order.'

But back he had to go to Kranz Kop where presently he received instructions to proceed to Rorke's Drift and camp there. This incident was cited in after days as proof of Durnford's insubordinate temperament. But is that quite reasonable? Does it not rather suggest that, under the conditions of native warfare, officers had usually been given a good deal of rope and had become accustomed, within limits, to take action on their own?

Durnford was naturally disappointed that his place was to be in the rear and not in the front of the advance; and he arrived at Rorke's Drift on January 20 in an unusually dejected mood. Next day he wrote his last letter, an unusually brief one, to his mother:

> I have sent on to ask for instructions from the general who is about ten miles off, forming a camp at or near the Isandhlwana mountain (see my map of Zululand). . . . This wet weather we have had is most depressing in every way, but today has been very hot, quite a pleasant change for me and, indeed, for all of us, black and white. The general has gone on with the first and second battalion of the 24th etc., and we follow on. I have no news, am stupid and dull, and "down," so *adieu* for the day. *P.S.* I am "down," because I'm *left behind*, (underlined in the original), but we shall see.

Meantime, the triple invasion had begun.

The Right Column started to cross the Tugela at daybreak on January 11th. The crossing was completed on the 13th, and work begun on building Fort Tenedos on the Zulu side of the river and stocking it with stores. On the 15th mounted troops reconnoitred some eight miles northwards. No Zulu forces were to be seen. On the 17th the fort was finished, and next day the column advanced. No opposition was encountered till, near the River Inyezane, on January 22, the column was attacked by some hundreds of Zulus. It easily repulsed them, and on January 23 it reached its objective at Eshowe, 37 miles from the Tugela. The building of another fort was at once begun, and preparations made for the next advance towards Ulundi, as soon as it were ordered.

Bodies of Zulus, meantime, had established themselves at various points round the camp. They did not attack: they watched and waited. It was not till January 28 that a messenger dipped through the tightening blockade with the long-awaited orders. They were not what Pearson had expected—not to advance, but to retreat, unless he felt quite safe where he was. 'You must be prepared to have the whole Zulu force down on you.' An entrenched *laager* was essential. No word of Isandhlwana; but it was clear enough that something had gone wrong. Five days later the bare news of a disaster got through.

Another five days, and the whole story was known. Thereafter no messengers were able to evade the Zulu sentinels: the investment was complete. But fortunately, Pearson had managed to bring up sufficient supplies, and the strength of his impromptu fortifications seemingly deterred the Zulus from risking an attack. In a few weeks' time communication was re-established by heliograph, and Pearson was informed of the date at which he might expect to be relieved. On March 29 Chelmsford crossed the Tugela at the head of a column of 3,400 white and 2,300 native troops. On April 2nd he put to flight a considerable Zulu force which barred his path at Gingihlovo. On the 3rd he

THE ATTEMPT TO SAVE THE COLOURS

reached Eshowe. It had been under siege of a sort for over ten weeks.

★★★★★★★★★★★★★★★★

The Left Column began to move from Bemba's Kop down the left bank of the Blood River on January 10th. Next day Wood rode ahead with a body of cavalry and met Chelmsford at a point some twelve miles from Rorke's Drift. As the result of decisions here taken, Wood's column moved back to Bemba's Kop, and waited there till the 18th, the day on which Pearson had begun to advance from the Tugela. Reconnaissance ahead was encouraging: no Zulus in force. On the 18th the column advanced to the Insegeni River and on the 20th reached the White Umvolosi near Chief Tinta's *kraal*. Tinta submitted and was dispatched with his people back to Utrecht. Next day a *laager*, reinforced with stone walls, was built—Fort Tinta—and in the early hours of the 32nd the column moved out towards the Zunguin Range. By sunset they had established an entrenched camp at the south-east end of it.

In the course of the day some 4,000 Zulus had been observed drilling, with admirable precision, on the north-west slope of Mount Inhlobane, the highest point of the range. As Wood and his men sat round their campfires that night, they heard the sound of guns away to the south-west. What that portended will appear as the narrative proceeds. On the 23rd the column remained halted at the camp. On the 24th it advanced eight miles northwards, a little beyond Mount Inhlobane, and was soon engaged with a body of Zulus.

It was not a large force and it was easily dispersed. But the advance was not continued; for during the skirmish a mounted messenger brought news of what had happened at Isandhlwana two days earlier. As soon as the fighting was over, therefore, and the troops had been given a rest, Wood started back to Fort Tinta. He reached it early on January 25th.

★★★★★★★★★★★★★★★★

The Central Column at Rorke's Drift was to cross the Buffalo on the same day (January 11th) as the Right Column crossed

BUFFALO RIVER TOWARDS FUGITIVE DRIFT

the Tugela. It dawned gloomily. A thick white fog descended in the early hours of the morning and presently turned to drizzling rain. But despite this handicap the passage of the Buffalo which began at 4.30 a.m. was earned out without loss—the British troops and most of the wagons and oxen crossing by the pontoons winch had been strung across the water on the previous day, the N.N.C. under Commandant Lonsdale by the ford where the river was running at six knots and rose at midstream to the men's chins.

The passage was covered by the guns which crossed with the rest of the wagons on the following day. Having gained the east bank, the infantry spread out in skirmishing order to a length of about three miles, advanced a few hundred yards up a gentle slope, and then halted to wait for better weather. No one yet knew whether, as had been rumoured, the Zulus meant to resist the invasion in force at once; but, when towards noon the fog lifted, there was not a Zulu to be seen.

Chelmsford, meanwhile, had ridden off with an escort of cavalry to that conference with Wood. He reported:

> We had a long talk together, and Wood arranged that he will occupy himself with the tribes on his front and left flank ... until we are ready to advance to Isipezi Hill. (25 miles east of Rorke's Drift).

On the ride out and back there was still no sign of Zulu forces. Groups of huts or *kraals* were visible here and there. A few armed Zulus were found in them and disarmed, and some hundreds of cattle, hones, sheep and goats were rounded up. Back in camp that afternoon, Chelmsford was visited by Durnford, riding over from Kranz Kop. He reported that 'all the fighting Zulus have gone away from the border' towards Ulundi. Chelmsford writes:

> This may be true, but *I shall make sure as I advance that we are not leaving any large force in our rear.* (Author's italics).

He told Wood:

We must try and push everyone slowly before us towards the king's *kraal*.

Next day (January 12th) the column had its first brush with the enemy. Reconnoitring in full strength along the eastward route it was presently to take, it came, some five miles out, to a rocky *kranz* near the *kraal* of Chief Sirayo, whose name has figured on an earlier page. Shots were fired at the column from caves in the *kranz*, whereupon the infantry opened out and attacked in attended order. The Zulus defended their position fiercely, firing from cover and rolling rocks down on their attackers as they climbed the slope. But in half an hour the fighting was over. The caves were occupied, the Zulus dispersed. Rounding up the cattle, the column returned to its base. Chelmsford reported to Frere:

> I ordered Sirayo's *kraal* to be burnt, but none of the other huts were touched. The Native Contingent behaved very well and not a native touched a woman or child or killed a wounded man.

The casualties had been small. About 30 Zulus killed on the one side; only three natives on the other.

> The country is in a terrible state from the rain, and I do not know how we shall, manage to get our troops across the valley, near Sirayo's *kraal*. . . . The soldiers are in excellent health and spirits and do not seem to feel, either physically or morally, the continuous duckings they get from the daily thunderstorms.

Sirayo's tribesmen had been only a handful, and there was still nothing to betray the whereabouts of the Zulu Army. C. L. Norris Newman, special correspondent of the *London Standard* and the only journalist accompanying the column, climbed to the top of the hill above the *kranz*.

> The sight obtained was magnificent. Looking north, down a precipitous cliff, a splendid valley extended for miles, rich in verdure, covered with deserted *kraals*, and

Views of Isandlwana

bounded on each side by high mountains; while to the south the Buffalo and the Natal mountains were seen in the distance, with our camp at Rorke's Drift looking like a tin miniature soldier's camp. To the eastward, the Isipezi Hill rose in the air with its curious-shaped head, and close beside it was *our road to Ulundi*. Altogether it was a sight worth seeing.

If Newman had stood there ten days later, the sight would have been the same: but, though the watcher would not have known it, somewhere out there, concealed by hills or in folds of undulating ground, Cetewayo's *impi* would by then have been lying in wait.

For the next few days, the column stayed in its camp near Rorke's Drift while a working party built a road across the soggy ground of the Bashee valley. On January 17 Chelmsford rode out along the Ulundi track to choose a site for his next camp. About seven miles, as the crow flies, from the *drift*, the track climbed some three hundred feet to a *col* between Isandhlwana mount and a rock-strewn ridge known as Stony Hill, and then descended to a plain, about eight miles long from east to west, and five miles broad from north to south.

★★★★★★★★★★

The Zulu word '*Isandhlwana*' has been variously construed as meaning 'little hand' or 'little house' or 'the lesser stomach of a cow.' The shape of the mount has been likened to that of a crouching lion, and officers of the 44th Regiment observed at the time its resemblance to the Sphinx in their regimental badge.

★★★★★★★★★★

It is slightly undulating, but more or less bare of trees. Viewed from Isandhlwana, the most striking feature is a queer conical *kopje* about 2,400 yards distant from the mount. Isandhlwana stands at the north-west corner of this plain, a bare block of sandstone, its curved crest rising to about 4,000 feet above sea-level, 500 above the level of the plain. Its length at the base, running N.N.E. to S.S.W. is about 500 yards, its breadth about 300.

From the *col* beside it the track to Ulundi led down to and across the plain south-eastwards. After four miles it bent due east and then climbed gradually to higher ground, while another native track, leading to the Qudeni Bush, continued south-eastwards down the plain towards the Malagata Hills.

It was on the slope leading up to the eastern side of Isandhlwana that Chelmsford decided to pitch his camp. Immediately behind it rose the steep wall of rock. In front lay the plain cut by several small dry streambeds and, some 2,000 yards away, by a fair-sized *donga*. Not much farther east rose the first of the undulating ridges behind which the track to Ulundi disappeared. Southwards the view lay open over most of the plain to the Malagatas. It was only on the north that the range of vision was dangerously narrow. Not far from the mount, the ground rose fairly steeply to a grassy plateau, stretching away and falling slightly for three or four miles towards the Ngutus, a range of mountains rising at its highest to 5,060 feet above sea-level.

Thus, for the camp at Isandhlwana the edge of this plateau was the sky-line: for it was about 500 feet higher than the camp, or approximately the same height as the mount. It ran roughly west to east, so that it was nearest to the mount—about 2,000 yards away—at a point due north of it. Just at this point, moreover, a broad sloping *spur* led down towards the mount. Between the foot of this *spur* and the mount was a more or less level stretch of about 1,000 yards.

The defensive strength of the position was obvious enough. Its rear was protected by the mount.

★★★★★★★★★★

Not impregnably, unless a guard were stationed on the summit Away from its precipitous southern end the mount can easily be climbed. When the author visited the site (December 39, 1947), an athletic member of his party reached the top from the *col* in seven minutes, another older member in fifteen.

★★★★★★★★★★

It commanded most of the plain. Its weakness lay in the fact that it was itself commanded at close quarters on the north. But it must not be forgotten that the British could not, like the Zulus, march freely across country: they were obliged to keep to the native track to Ulundi, improving it as they advanced; and it is at least doubtful if a better position was to be found near the track within a day's march from the base. A subordinate reason for the choice was that brushwood for the camp-fires was available where the track climbed the western slope.

Early on the morning of January 20th, leaving one company of the 2/24th with a few engineers and some native troops to guard the *drift*, the column started, 'the bands playing merrily,' on its march to Isandhlwana. From time to time, it was held up by the bad condition of the track. At one point a stream had to be bridged with rocks and the approaches cut away and levelled. But Isandhlwana was readied about midday and in the course of the afternoon the camp was pitched.

Chelmsford's tents were set up at the foot of the rock-strewn slope below the mount The troops were stationed parallel with the mount, at about 150 yards' distance from it, with the wagons and oxen in their rear. On the left, nearest the plateau, were the second and first battalions of the 3rd N.N.C. and then, in order to the right, the 2/24th, the six R A guns, the colonial mounted infantry, the Natal mounted police, and, last, the 1/24th. The line extended some 250 yards beyond the mount, so that the colonial troops and the 1/24th were on the slope below the *col* and Stony Hill.

That afternoon, while the camp was settling down, Chelmsford rode out with a small mounted force across the plain to examine the high ground at its south-eastern end. No Zulus were seen. Before sunset he was back in camp.

4

The controversy which the impending disaster inevitably excited was to exhibit much smug 'wisdom after the event.' But there was one question at least which it was fair to ask *post eventum*. Why was the camp not protected as strongly as possible against the risk of sudden attack?

The minimum precautions against surprise were taken as a

matter of course. Pickets were posted in an arc covering the front and both flanks of the camp at a distance of 2,000 yards, and vedettes (mounted patrols) were sent out to one or two points on the edge of the plateau and out on the plain. Apparently, no look-out was posted on the top of the mount. At night, the line of sentinels, except for one outpost on the north, was withdrawn to 500 yards from the camp. On the *col* itself a permanent guard of the 1/24th was posted day and night. So far so good: but that was all. Nothing was done to fortify, however modestly, the camp itself. And this seems, at first sight, a strange omission. For, if one lesson more than another had been taught by experience of native warfare in South Africa, it was the danger of surprise attack; and the Boers, who, ever since the Great Trek, had been constantly fighting the natives, had devised, as has been explained above, an effective method of defence.

To form a *laager* had long been a regular, an almost automatic, precaution for Boers in the field, and in the regulations issued to the British forces as late as the previous November officers were instructed that, at night, oxen and horses should always be tethered in wagon *laagers*. As it happened, the need for taking this essential precaution was urged on Chelmsford by two Boers who certainly knew what they were talking about. When he was at Pietermaritzburg, preparing for the invasion, Paul Kruger was taken to see by the Rev. George Stegmann, a minister of the Dutch Reformed Church, who acted as interpreter and secretary to Frere. The minister noted in his diary:

> Mr. Kruger gave him (Chelmsford) much valuable information as to Zulu tactics and impressed upon him the absolute necessity of *laagering* his wagons every evening and always at the approach of the enemy. He also urged the necessity of scouting at considerable distances, as the movements of the Zulus were very rapid.

Similar advice was given by Paul Beater who had fought under Pretorius; and an unsuccessful attempt was made on the eve of the invasion to obtain the services of a 'colonial' who had had experience of forming *laagers*. But Chelmsford thought—so he afterwards explained—that a *laager* should serve not as a 'bastion' but only to prevent the baggage animals from being stampeded and cut off. In any case, he pointed out, at Isandhlwana a *laager* could have been formed only at night, since in daytime the wagons were wanted to fetch up more stores from Rorke's Drift. Many of the wagons had not in fact reached the camp before nightfall on the 20th, and those that had were busy unloading.

So much for the *laager*, but there was another instruction in the regulations. 'The camp should be partially entrenched on all sides.' If that order had been obeyed at Isandhlwana, a shallow trench—deep trenching was almost impossible in such stony ground—would presumably have been dug, at least at intervals, along the front and round both flanks and also on the crest of the *col* where the rear was not defended by the mount; and, trench or no trench, a breastwork of rocks could have been built, sufficient to protect troops, lying down or kneeling, from rifle-shots and flying *assegais*. But the instruction was not obeyed. It was afterwards explained that the troops had only arrived in the course of the afternoon, that they were tired out by their hard day's work, and that the sun set soon after six p.m. Thus the camp's sole defence was the great rampart that shielded most but not all of its rear.

In the days to come, when every detail of the catastrophe had been threshed out, the omission to fortify the camp emerged from the dust of controversy as the one unquestionable blunder. But it is fair to remember that Isandhlwana was intended to be no more than a temporary resting-place; that the first post where stores were to be collected and preparations made for the next stage of the advance was Isipezi, some twelve miles farther on; and that the column was expected to strike camp as soon as the forward track had been reconnoitred and improved. Moreover—and this is the cardinal point—there was no reason to suppose, at the time the camp was pitched, that it was in any danger of a surprise attack by larger Zulu forces than could easily be repelled by guns and rifle fire on open ground.

There were still no Zulus to be seen, it was not yet certain even that they intended to resist the invasion. In any case it was believed—and rightly on January 20th—that no large body of Zulus had gathered to the north of the camp. The vedettes were out on the high ground and had nothing to report. It was thought too—and again rightly—that, if resistance had been decided on, the base of the Zulu advance would be Cetewayo's *kraal* at Ulundi. And it was assumed—not so rightly—that an *impi* moving from the direction of Ulundi towards Isandhlwana was bound to be detected long before it came to close-quarters.

5

The first evening at Isandhlwana camp was cheerful. Convinced that there was no large Zulu force in the immediate vicinity, Chelmsford had decided to prepare for his next move by probing the country towards Isipezi. If the Zulus were intending to bar his way to Ulundi, it was in that direction he expected to find them. He gave orders, therefore, for a reconnaissance in force next day towards Chief Matyana's *kraal* in the Mangeni valley among the hills that close in the plain to the south-east. The news was warmly welcomed in the camp.

Nearly everybody, wrote the journalist, wanted to join the party, but those who were to be left behind consoled themselves with the belief that the whole column would soon be involved in a major action, The Zulu *impi*, it was rumoured, was marching from Ulundi straight towards them. 'Our mess had a jolly little dinner that evening.'

At dawn next day (January 21st) the reconnoitring force set out along the track across the plain. It consisted of most of the N.N.C.—eight out of ten companies from each of its two battalions—under Commandant Lonsdale, followed later on by most of the mounted troops under Major Dartnell. The journalist who accompanied the outgoing force recalled:

How well I remember that morning, and the dejected aspect of the officers detained by duty at the camp! Young Buée, the assistant surgeon, started with us, but his pony went so lame that he was obliged to go back, unhappily as it turned out . . .

Chelmsford stayed behind. In the morning he rode out towards Maiagata mountain to a point whence the valley into which the N.N.C. had descended was visible, but nothing could be seen of them. Early in the afternoon a message came back from Dartnell reporting that he had linked up with Lonsdale and his N.N.C., and that some 400 Zulus were posted ahead of him, and asking for instructions, Chelmsford sent orders to attack at discretion. Later in the day he rode up to a point on the plateau where some vedettes were posted. Fourteen mounted Zulus were observed near the Ngutus about four miles away. They presently disappeared. Two of the vedettes said they had seen these Zulus several times during the day. Seemingly a mere patrol. There was no sign or hint of the presence of larger forces anywhere.

It was the same with the reconnoitring force marching southeast that morning. The countryside seemed to have been depopulated. Traces of recent occupation were observed in deserted *kraals*, but no Zulus were visible till, soon after midday, Dartnell approached the mountains. Then, as he informed Chelmsford, a few hundred Zulus were seen. About four o'clock mounted scouts reported that some 1,500 Zulus were holding a rocky *col* a few miles to the east. The N.N.C. thereupon advanced to the crest of the first low range whence massed Zulus, some 2,000 strong, were observed on the next range across a shallow valley. A small mounted force was dispatched to test the position. One of them related:

> Then appeared, as if by magic, from one end of the ridge to the other, a long line of black men in skirmishing order, advancing at a run. It was a grand sight, and they never uttered a sound. I defy the men of any British regiment to keep their intervals so well at the double. On reaching the brow of the hill, the centre halted and the Horns appeared.

The troops retired to avoid encirclement, but they were not pursued. The Zulus stopped and then withdrew. It looked as if they wanted to lure their enemies after them up into the hills.

It was now near sunset, and Dartnell, so some critics afterwards asserted, should have recognised that his orders to reconnoitre had now been carried out and should have at once marched back to the camp. But in consultation with his fellow officers, he had decided to bivouac for the night on the spot and attack the Zulus next morning. Hs sent off, accordingly, a report to Chelmsford, describing the situation and asking for food and blankets to be sent out to him that night and reinforcements on the morrow.

It might almost seem as if Dartnell had taken charge of the whole operation and was forcing Chelmsford's hand. For his orders were to return to the camp after completing his reconnaissance. But Chelmsford, though 'much vexed' (he afterwards said) at Dartnell's disobedience, complied with his request.

Biscuit and blankets were dispatched that night. At 1.30 next morning (January 22nd), Chelmsford received another message saying that the Zulus were in great force. That was not, in fact, the case. The Zulus attacked by Dartnell, it afterwards appeared, were only a body of Chief Matyana's tribesmen marching to join the main *impi* which was then, as will be seen, a few miles away near Isipezi, But Chelmsford seems to have supposed—and it was not unreasonable—that the main *impi* was the great force immediately in front of Dartnell. In any case he thought it necessary to go to Dartnell's support in strength if only to prevent the N.N.C. from suffering a reverse which might so wreck their morale as to make them useless for the rest of the campaign.

So, before dawn, more than half of the troops at Isandhlwana—seven companies of the 2/24th, a squadron of horse, and four guns under Colonel Harness—set out up the plain, accompanied by the general in person. Before leaving he sent orders to Durnford to move his troops at once to the camp, where they would compensate to some extent for the loss of the force now leaving it. Colonel Pulleine was left in command of the camp with orders to stay and protect it.

Chelmsford's force reached Dartnell's position soon after

MUSICIANS OF THE 24TH

daybreak and found the mountains still cloaked in mist When it rose, no Zulu Army was revealed. Though many camp fires had been burning in the night on the opposite ridge, only one or two outposts were now to be seen. The *impi*, if such it was, had completely disappeared. But it was supposed that it had withdrawn behind the outposts, and presently a body of Zulus was seen advancing to take possession of an outstanding *spur* of the ridge Chelmsford decided on a combined advance in the hope of surrounding the whole Zulu position.

The N.N.C. were ordered to make a frontal attack on the hill, with Dartnell and the colonial mounted troops on their right, while farther north the guns under flames, the 2/24th, and the mounted infantry threatened the Zulu right flank. The Zulus making for the *spur* fell back before this advance. Other small bodies were encountered and easily dispersed. It was believed that the *impi* still lay ahead, and the advance was continued towards Isipezi Hill some six miles distant. At 9.30 a.m. Chelmsford and his staff halted for breakfast.

Just at this time a brief message arrived from Pulleine:

Report just come in that the Zulus are advancing in force from the left front of the camp (8.5).

It was puzzling news, since the area to the left, *i.e.,* to the north of Isandhlwana, was thought to be empty of Zulus. So, Chelmsford sent Lieutenant Milne (afterwards Admiral Sir Berkely Milne, Bt.), to the top of a neighbouring hill from which the camp could be seen ten miles away. He stayed there over an hour looking at the camp through 'a very powerful telescope.' He reported 'nothing unusual,' 'no sign of an enemy near Isandhlwana.' Chelmsford concluded, therefore, that all was well; but, before continuing his advance, he ordered one battalion of the N.N.C. under Commandant Browne to return to the camp and make sure on the way that no scattered parties of Zulus were threatening his line of communication with it.

At that moment, though Chelmsford could not know it, the last chance of saving the situation passed away. If, instead of those few N.N.C., the whole of the mounted troops and the guns had been sent back to Isandhlwana at full speed, they would have been just in time.

As the morning drew on, since the advancing troops were unable to come to grips with the Zulus who continued to withdraw before them, Chelmsford decided to halt the forward movement. His plan, it will be remembered, was to advance stage by stage along the track towards Ulundi, pushing the Zulus in front of him, and protecting his flanks from encirclement, He was convinced that there were no substantial Zulu forces in his rear, and he was confronted by what seemed to be the main *impi* from Ulundi.

He decided therefore to concentrate his whole column at a new forward camp. Having selected a site for it at the head of the Mangeni valley, he ordered the troops engaged that day to withdraw to it, and at the same time dispatched Captain Gardiner to the old camp with orders for Pulleine to strike the tents and load up the baggage of all the troops that had so far marched out eastwards and to send them on to the new camp that very afternoon together with rations and forage for seven days.

★★★★★★★★★★

The note conveying those orders was lost in the battle. The gist of it was reported by Capt. Gardiner from memory in a statement dated, Jan. 26, in which he added to the orders quoted in the text an order telling Pulleine to 'remain himself at his present camp and entrench it.' This additional order was not mentioned in the evidence given by Gardiner at the Court of Inquiry on Jan. 27: and, in view of Chelmsford's conviction as to the position of the *impi*, it was doubtful if the order was actually given.

★★★★★★★★★★

Presumably Chelmsford intended that this force, together with has own headquarters, should follow the main body of the column in due course, only such a detachment being left behind as might be necessary to safeguard communication with Rorke's Drift.

At midday Chelmsford was at the site he had chosen. Isandhlwana could be seen from a hill beside it, and, looking through their field-glasses, staff officers observed some large bodies of Zulus not far from the camp. But Chelmsford was not at all alarmed. He was quite confident that Pulleine's troops, presumably reinforced by now by Durnford's—a total strength of over 1,700 men, half of them British, with guns and rockets, posted on ground he thought well-suited for defence—could beat off any such Zulu forces *as could possibly have gathered in the neighbourhood at that time.* And, naturally enough, this confidence was not shaken when it presently appeared that some sort of attack, was actually afoot.

About 12.15 p.m. some Zulu prisoners were brought in and questioned by Chelmsford's interpreter. They said that a great *impi* was coming that day from Ulundi. If their enumeration of the regiments was correct, it was a large force, upwards of 20,000 men. But there was nothing surprising or disturbing in that. A Zulu advance in full strength was to be expected. Such a concentration of his own forces as Chelmsford had just decided on was the way to meet it. But, while the prisoners were being cross-examined, came the sound, distinct and unmistakable, of cannon-fire from the direction of Isandhlwana.

'Do you hear that?' exclaimed the Zulus. 'There is fighting going on at the camp.'

About an hour later, a mounted native came galloping down from a neighbouring ridge. He had seen the smoke of battle at the camp; he said. Chelmsford and his staff at once rode up the hill. Field-glasses were levelled again on Isandhlwana. It was a sunny day, and the bright trim rows of tents were plainly visible. Men were moving about among them. Nothing odd in that. There was no sign of commotion, still less of fighting. How were the watchers to know that, actually within the last hour, a terrible disaster had occurred? If a Zulu attack had been made on the camp—and that, it seemed, was what the firing must have meant—it had evidently been repulsed.

Only those, few officers who happened to be nearer to Isandhlwana knew better. One of them, Captain Church of the

2/24th, related afterwards how he had been with the guns under Colonel Harness on their way to the new site when cannon-fire was heard from the vicinity of the old camp, some eight miles off, and, looking in that direction, they:

> . . . .saw shells bursting against the hills to the left of it (*i.e.* the plateau). We did not know what to make of this, and were puzzled how to act, when about one o'clock a body of about 1,000 natives suddenly appeared in the plain below and between us and the camp.

Church rode down to find out who they were, and was met by a galloping messenger. That body of natives, it appeared, was Browne's battalion of the N.N.C. which Chelmsford had dispatched back towards Isandhlwana earlier in the day. The horseman was bearing a message from Browne—a message as horrifying as it was utterly unexpected, it ran:

> For God's sake come back, the camp is surrounded.

In the report he submitted later on, Browne said that he had received the order to return to Isandhlwana about 10 a.m. and that he had not gone far before a Zulu scout was caught who declared that an *impi* was about to attack the camp. He sent off a messenger to take this information to Chelmsford. A mile or two farther, large bodies of Zulus could be seen in the neighbourhood of the camp. Another message was dispatched to that effect. Because Chelmsford could not be found or for some other reason, neither of these two messages reached him.

Browne, meantime, had come within full view of Isandhlwana. Heavy fighting was going on around the camp. He saw one of the guns alter position and fire towards the front of the camp. Soon after that the guns ceased firing. It was impossible for Browne to go to the rescue with his N.N.C., even if it had not been too late. His way was barred by a mass of Zulus who seemed to be manoeuvring to attack him. Despatching that desperate message, he began to retreat.

Church spurred back with the news to Harness, whom he

found in conversation with Chelmsford's senior A.D.C., Major Gossett Harness at once decided to make at full speed for Isandhlwana; but Gossett, who seems to have shared his chief's sense of security to the full, discouraged the idea. Harness, however, insisted, and Gossett rode off to Chelmsford with Harness' report that he was going to the rescue of the camp. Before long he was back again with instructions that Harness was to carry out his original orders and march to the new site.

This is one of the strangest incidents in the strange story of that day. Did Gossett give Chelmsford Harness' message? Was he told of Browne's desperate appeal? If so, the impregnability of the camp must have now become such an *idée fixe* in his mind that he disregarded it. In any case the recall of Harness was of no practical importance. All was over at Isandhlwana long before he could have got his guns there.

About 2 pm Chelmsford decided to return to his headquarters under the mount. An hour later, as he and his staff were riding slowly back towards Isandhlwana, two messages met them from the camp, reporting that, since fighting had begun on the left of the camp, the order to shift part of it could not yet be carried out. These messages were addressed to staff officers and were apparently not passed on at once to Chelmsford.

★★★★★★★★★★

Speaking in the House of Lords (Septembers, 1880) Chelmsford said that only one message from the camp was received by him that day, *i.e.* the first message despatched by Pulleine about 8 a.m.

★★★★★★★★★★

If they had been, it may be taken for granted that they would have caused him no more serious uneasiness than they caused his staff. After all, the messengers could not have left the camp much later than midday—in fact they had lost some time in trying to find the general—and had they not, all of them, looked at the camp themselves about 1.15 p.m. and seen no sign of trouble? Was this not just another intimation that an attack had indeed been made between noon and one p.m., and had, if they could trust their eyesight, been repulsed? The little party rode on at a leisurely pace. 'The horses had had a hard day's work,' said one of their riders afterwards. At 3.30 p.m. the camp was still some five miles off. Then, suddenly, the blow fell. A man was seen approaching on a stumbling pony. It was Lonsdale and he brought black news. The Zulus were in possession of the camp.

Lonsdale, it appeared, had lost touch with his battalion of N.N.C., in pursuit of a mounted Zulu, and, finding himself alone, had ridden quietly back to Isandhlwana to prepare for the return of his men to what, so far as he was aware, was still their base. He was hot and tired. He had no suspicion of danger, and he did not trouble to keep a sharp look-out. The tents could be seen some miles away, and moving spots of scarlet among them betrayed the presence of the 'redcoats.' As he drew nearer, he was fired on by a Zulu sentinel. Even that did not open his eyes. He thought it was a careless native. He rode on, still half-asleep.

He was actually within ten yards of the tents when he became suddenly aware of the appalling, the incredible truth. Those red coats covered black bodies. There was no white man to be seen. A Zulu warrior stepped out from a tent close by. Wheeling his pony Lonsdale galloped off, the bullets whistling round him. He had escaped death by a hairsbreadth. If the Zulus had not been busy looting the camp, he could not have escaped at all. If they had cared, to pursue him, they must have caught him; for his pony, out all day, was now near the end of its strength. As soon as he was out of range, he had to dismount and lead it. It took him more than an hour to cover the five miles to the point at which Chelmsford met him.

There could be no mistaking the truth this time, and Chelmsford was dumbfounded. 'I can't understand it,' he exclaimed: 'I left a thousand men there.' But he kept his head and took immediate decisions. Riders were dispatched to countermand the concentration at the new camp and to order all the troops and the guns to retire as fast as possible towards Isandhlwana. Chelmsford himself advanced with the N.N.C. strung out in line and mounted infantry on either flank, till he was about three miles distant from the old camp.

There, concealed from it by a ridge of ground, he halted to wait for Glyn and Harness and the rest to catch him up. Meantime he sent out patrols to get as close a view of the camp as they could. The Zulus, they reported, were swarming like bees about it, swarming, too, all along the plain and upon the hills. The sun was setting by the time the whole force had arrived and been formed up in order of advance—the guns in the centre, three companies of the 2/24th on each side, the native troops on the flanks. At 6.30 p.m. the column, every man in it now aware that a shocking catastrophe had occurred, moved off into the gathering dusk.

6

What had happened that day at Isandhlwana? How had the Zulus managed to concentrate such an overwhelming force upon the camp?

Their advantage over the British forces in mobility has already been pointed out. They could move across any sort of terrain almost at horse speed. But they had another and even greater advantage—in 'intelligence.' Chelmsford knew nothing of Zulu movements beyond a radius of a very few miles. They could move in mass by night and hide by day in folds of the undulating countryside. Even at close range large numbers could lie concealed in *dongas* and *kranzes* or in long grass.

British patrols, unused to native warfare, could scarcely be blamed if they looked across a league of landscape which in fact contained thousands of Zulus and saw no sign of life in it. To the Zulus, on the other hand, whose fast-moving spies were scattered far and wide, every move the British made was plain to see. It may be taken for granted that their commanders had early information of the triple invasion and the direction of each, column's advance.

Their strategic plan can be inferred with reasonable certainty from what took place and from the subsequent statements of prisoners in British hands. From the main base at Ulundi two subsidiary holding forces were dispatched to confront the Left and Right Columns. The major force, from 25,000 to 30,000 strong, moved straight towards the Central Column. Certainly, they did not contemplate a defensive strategy. They had no artillery; their firearms were relatively few and mostly antiquated flint-locks. Their strength was in the *assegai* and the traditional long-practised advance of the terrible Chest and Horns. When and where they came to grips with the Central Column would depend, of course, on circumstances. They would try to catch it at a disadvantage.

But one part of their plan is clear. They intended to take up a position, undetected, on the column's left flank. Thence, outnumbering it as they did by six or seven to one, they might try to surround it. Or they could strike at its rear first, cutting its communications with Rorke's Drift. Or, applying the same tactics on a wider scale, they could invade Natal.

By the evening of January 20th, when the Central Column was settling down in its new camp at Isandhlwana, the first stage of this Zulu plan had been carried out. The minor Zulu forces lay some distance ahead of the Right and Left Columns. The main force, which had left Ulundi on the 17th with orders to march west by easy stages, had arrived at Isipesi Hill. They had seen some mounted white men away to their left that afternoon, evidently Chelmsford and his reconnoitring force. So, though Chelmsford had not seen them, he was right in thinking that the *impi* was probably somewhere in that neighbourhood at that time. But on the 21st the whole strategic situation changed.

The Zulu spies must have reported the arrival of Dartnell's troops at the head of the plain at dawn. Plainly that meant that the strength of the column at Isandhlwana had been to that extent reduced; and in the course of the day, leaving Dartnell to do what he liked, the *impi*, regiment by regiment, stole off to take up quite a new position. 'Keeping away to the eastward,' as those Zulu prisoners explained, and so concealed by the high ground on that side of the plain, they made for the eastern flank of the Ngutus.

When Chelmsford rode out northwards of the camp that afternoon, they must have been well on their way. Before sunset they had reached their objective, a rocky, bushy valley close under the north-east slope of the Ngutus about five miles from Isandhlwana and, of course, completely hidden from it. (Local tradition puts the valley near what is now Cadworth Farm).

There they spent the night. They made no noise. They lit no fires. . . . Next morning their spies on the edge of the plateau brought good news. Not only had Dartnell's force remained some miles up the plain, but in the early hours half the remaining troops in the camp had marched out to join it. A message could reach the Zulus facing Dartnell in an hour or so, and possibly they were told to retreat and try to draw the British after them farther and farther from the camp.

'No doubt,' said Milne (the young staff-officer with the telescope) after the event, 'the force we were after was a blind.' But, whether the Zulu withdrawal at the southern end of the plain was deliberate or not, the tactical result of Chelmsford's advance thither with Glyn's troops was evident enough to the Zulu watchers on the crest at its northern end. 'You gave us the battle,' said an *induna* afterwards, 'by splitting up into small parties.'

That day, however, the Zulus did not intend to attack the camp. It was the day of the new moon, a 'dark' unlucky day. The assault was to be made at dawn or earlier next morning. Outposts would be stationed on the higher ground. A detachment might move across the plateau south-westwards so as to threaten the rear of the camp and its communicators with Rorke's Drift. The rest of the host would lie waiting for the morrow in their secluded valley.

7

It was not till about 8 a.m. on the 22nd that Pulleine became aware of the presence of Zulus to the northward of his camp. A picket of the N.N.C., returning from night duty on the *spur*, reported that a body of Zulus was moving across the plateau from the direction of the Ngutus. Thereupon Pulleine sent off a mes-

REFERENCE TABLE

A to B Site of Camp 22nd January 1879

1. 1-24th Regiment.
2. Natural Camp { Mounted Infantry, N.M.P, N.Gardeners and N.M.R }
3. Col. Harness's Battery.
4. 2-24th Regiment.
5. N.N.C.
6. N.N.C.

C Col. Durnford R.E , Capt. Wardell, 1-24th Reg't, Lieut. Dyer 2-24th Reg't, Lieut. Scott N.Carb'rs, Lieut. Bradstreet N.M.R , Quart'r Hitchcock N.M.R , 1 Officer 24th Reg't unrecognisable and about 110 men (mostly 24th Reg't) buried here

D Capt. R. Younghusband, 1-24th Reg't, 2 Officers 24th Reg't unrecognisable, and about 60 men (24th Reg't) buried here

E Black's Kopjie
About 100 white bodies buried on rock below, close to road; also many single bodies along road which runs at head of camp as for at B.

F Isandhlwana Rock

G to H Signs of heavy fighting and determined stand having been made here.
Kraal at G full of dead Zulus.
Color Serj't Wolf and 20 men (24th Reg't) found amongst rocks just above G.
The southern crest line from G to H strewn with empty cartridge cases
Guns of R.A. were firing for some time from point H to kraals at I which were afterwards found full of dead Zulus.

I Cairns

⌂ Kraals

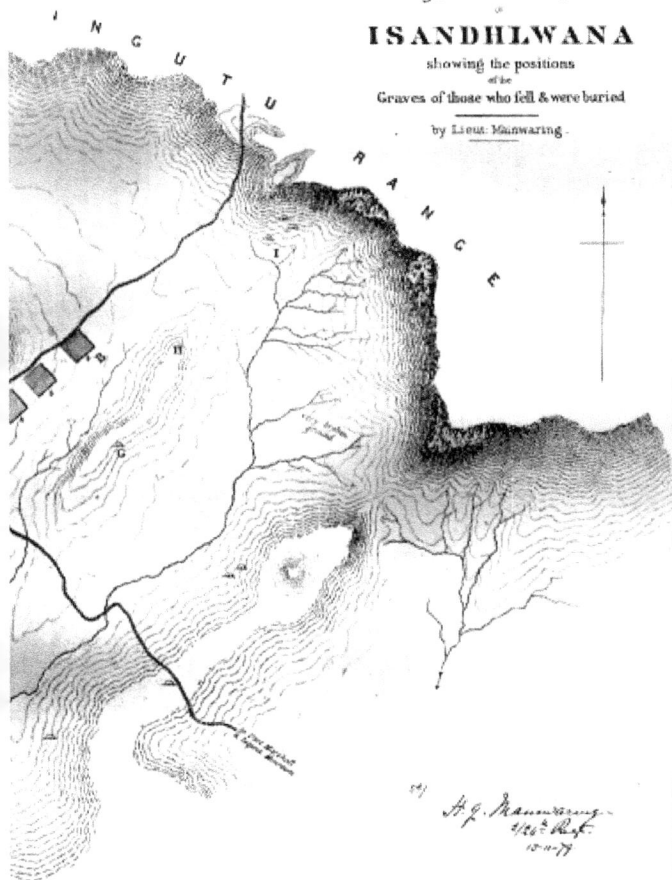

SKETCH MAP
of
ISANDHLWANA
showing the positions
of the
Graves of those who fell & were buried

by Lieut. Mainwaring.

INGUTU RANGE

sage to Chelmsford, held back the relief picket of the N.N.C. and called the rest of his troops to arms. Falling in before their tents, they were marched to a position covering the north-east corner of the camp. But no attack developed, and presently the troops were withdrawn to the ground in front of the tents and stood at ease.

About 9 a.m. Zulus were seen on the edge of the plateau; but they presently disappeared, and those seen an hour earlier were now said to be withdrawing. All was quiet. The troops remained at ease in their position. Nothing happened till about 10 a.m., when a runner from the N.N.C. picket which had resumed its station on the *spur*, reported Zulus again on the plateau. There were more of them this time, and they were moving westwards. A little later Durnford arrived at the head of his force.

The orders dispatched from Isandhlwana early that morning and signed 'J. N. C.' had reached Durnford at Rorke's Drift about 6 a.m.

> 22nd, Wednesday, 2 a.m., You are to march to this camp *at once* (original italics), with all the force you have with you of No. 2 Column. ... 2/24th, Artillery and mounted men with the general and Colonel Glyn move off at once to attack a Zulu force about ten miles distant'.

By 7.30 a.m., Durnford's little force was on the road to Isandhlwana. It consisted of some 300 Basuto horse, a rocket battery, commanded by Captain Russell, and two companies of the N.N.C. under Captains Nourse and Stafford, In the rear came the slow-moving ox-wagons. Nobody was seen till about ten, when, as the horsemen were breasting the slope to the *col*, they met Lieutenant Chard, R.E., who was stationed at Rorke's Drift and on his way back there from the camp. Zulus, he said, were visible on the plateau; and some of them were moving so far to the west that he was afraid they might make a dash for the *drift*.

Durnford asked Chard, as he rode down, to tell the officer commanding the rocket battery to hurry on, to put an extra guard on the wagons, and to bid the whole column to keep a sharp look-out on its left. When the Basutos reached the top of the *col*, the rocket battery and the two companies of the N.N.C. were close on their heels, but the wagons were not much more than half-way from the *drift*. So Durnford dispatched a troop of Basutos to strengthen their small escort of native foot.

On arrival at the camp Durnford, since he was senior to Pulleine, took over the command from him, and with the command, of course, the general's order to defend the camp. (See Note A). His first concern was Chard's report of Zulus on the plateau. No further information had come in from the *spur* due north of the camp; so, he ordered some natives to climb the mount and send down word of what could be seen from the top. Then the two officers repaired to Pulleine's tent for a quick early lunch. In the course of the meal a series of reports came in from the outposts on the *spur*. 'The enemy are in force behind the hills to the left. . .' 'The enemy are in three columns. . . .' 'The columns are separating, one moving to the left rear and one towards the general. . .'

The last message came from the top of the mount 'The enemy are retreating in all directions.' Were these large forces or no more than strong patrols or forage parties? Durnford decided to go out and 'follow them up,' and in particular to head off that body of them which was said to be moving 'towards the general' and prevent it from linking up with the *impi* which everyone at the camp believed to be confronting Chelmsford at the other end of the plain.

Since the Zulus might be in some strength, he proposed to take out the whole of his own force; but, apart from the gunners of the rocket-battery, it was a purely native force, and to provide it with a stiffening of white troops, he asked Pulleine if he could spare him two companies of the 24th. It is a natural human tendency to dramatise the prelude to a disaster after it has occurred, and the most circumstantial rumours were afoot a few days later to the effect that Durnford and Pulleine had quarrelled on this question of the two companies. 'High words,' it was said, 'were exchanged.'

There was not a grain of truth, in this. Lieutenant Cochrane, a member of Durnford's staff, was present during the conversation and afterwards reported it, as far as memory would serve, written. 'The manner of the officers to one another was perfectly genial and courteous.' Pulleine demurred to Durnford's request for the companies in view of his orders to defend the camp.

'But the Zulus are retiring,' said Durnford.

'Very well,' replied Pulleine; 'if you order it. I'll give you them.'

But Durnford refused to take the high hand. He gave in. He would go without the white men; but if he got into difficulties, he would count on Pulleine to help him out.

Durnford's first move was to dispatch two troops of Basutos, each about 50 strong, to climb the plateau at the nearest point and scout along it to the cast The rocket-battery and the two companies of the N.N.C. having now arrived, he ordered them to support his advance. Then he himself led out the rest of his Basutos eastward across the plain, passing to the south of the conical *kopje*. Between eleven o'clock and noon these operations were being carried out as planned. The Basutos climbed the plateau and spread out over it. No Zulus were seen at first, only a herd of cattle. The Basutos rode on to round it up.

Presently they came to the brink of a valley, and saw, about a mile off, what they had never dreamed of seeing. Thousands of Zulus were gathered there. Most of them were sitting on the ground, taking their ease. One body was moving westwards, probably taking up position to encircle the north flank of the camp at the appointed time. But the sudden sight of the Basutos trespassing so near at hand precipitated the mass attack that was to have been withheld till after midnight.

The Zulus sprang to their feet. Shots were exchanged. The Basutos retreated. After them came a whole regiment of the *impi*; and, catching, as it were, the infection of their advance, up and out across the plateau came another regiment and another. The Battle of Isandhlwana had begun.

Durnford, meanwhile, bearing, to the left across the plain,

Private. 1879

had got some four miles from the camp and had cantered forward in advance of his Basutos when a vedette of the Natal Carabineers came galloping down from the plateau. There was a huge Zulu *impi* beyond the crest, he said; and, almost as he spoke, the first ranks of it were seen against the sky-line. No one who saw what followed and survived the day can ever have forgotten it. On and on they came, and more and more of them, till soon the whole green slope down to the plain was blackened out by one huge moving screen of Zulus.

The rocket-battery and the N.N.C. were the first to feel the weight of the attack. They had been left behind by Durnford's mounted force, and their efforts to catch, up with it had been impeded by the rocky ground, the mules had been unable to get across it with their loads, and the rocket-guns had been shifted to the shoulders of some twenty-five men of the N.N.C. They were still about two miles behind Durnford, and somewhat nearer than he was to the slope, when a *carabineer* galloped up with the news that the Basutos who had been sent out to patrol the plateau were in action beyond some rising ground on their left front. Russell at once rode up the rise and saw, not far away, the *impi* descending from the plateau.

Racing back, he ordered the rocket-guns into 'action front'; but at that moment a body of Zulus, who, with their usual capacity for concealment, had been lurking in a cleft, nearby, charged down on the battery's left flank. And then, when only one rocket had been fired, 'the Zulus,' said a private who survived, 'came over the hill in masses.' The mules stampeded. Most of the N.N.C. fled.

★★★★★★★★★★

'I observed that a great many of them,' Private Johnson recorded afterwards, 'were unable to extract the empty cartridge-cases after firing, and offered to do so for some of them, but they would not give me their rifles.'

★★★★★★★★★★

Russell was shot. But Nourse held on. He had only four men left out of 120 when Durnford came to his rescue.

At the first sight of the oncoming host Durnford galloped back to his Basutos, and, throwing them out in skirmishing line, he steadily retreated, halting from time to time to turn and fire on the advancing Zulus. Those who were attacking the rocket battery made no attempt to intercept him. They seem to have halted or withdrawn, so that the survivors of the battery, whose fate had hitherto been concealed from Durnford by the rising ground, were saved.

It was impossible to salvage the rocket-guns and ammunition—the main Zulu advance was now too near—and Durnford had to continue his slow retreat until he reached the big *donga* running parallel with the front of the camp and about a mile distant from its right flank. There he was reinforced by thirty or forty Colonial Horse. It was a strong position. The bank of the *donga* offered shelter to men firing over its lip. He decided to make a stand there.

It was now about 12.15 p.m. What had happened in the last half-hour at the camp?

When Durnford set off down across the plain, Pulleine, it seems, had been infected by his suspicion that there *might* be Zulus in some strength to the northward. At any rate he did something to meet a possible threat to the left flank of the camp. He sent out one company of the 1/24th about 1,200 yards to the *spur* leading up to the plateau. That seemed enough; the rest of the troops were dismissed and returned to the camp where they enjoyed the quiet of a sunny morning.

Nothing disturbing happened for an hour or so. The cooks were busy preparing the midday meal. How little danger was suspected and how suddenly it came may be shown by one personal experience. Captain Essex of the 75th, one of the few survivors, wrote three days later as follows.

Wishing to write some letters and thinking everything was now quiet, I went to my tent and was soon busy with my papers. About noon a sergeant came into my tent and told me that firing was to be heard behind the hill where the company of the 1/24th had been sent. I had my glasses over my shoulder and thought I might as well take my revolver, but did not trouble to put on my sword, as I thought nothing of the matter and expected to be back in half an hour to complete my letters.

Just at the time at which that firing was heard—it must have been the beginning of the Basutos skirmish on the plateau—two horsemen galloped up from opposite directions. One was Captain G. Shepstone, who had been with the Basutos on the plateau, to report that the Zulus were coming in great force. The other was Captain Gardiner with those orders from the general that the tents and baggage of all the troops out in the field with him should be sent on forthwith. It was an order, Gardiner pointed out at once, which in the circumstances could not be obeyed. Pulleine agreed and sent a horseman back to Chelmsford with a terse message addressed 'Staff Officer.'

Heavy firing to the left of our camp. Cannot move camp at present.

★★★★★★★★★★

A little later, Gardiner dispatched a message to Major Clery, on Chelmsford's staff. 'Heavy firing near left of camp. Shepstone has come in for reinforcements and reports that Zulus are falling back. The whole force at camp turned out and fighting about one mile to left flank.'

★★★★★★★★★★

Then Pulleine sounded the 'fall in' and the men came tumbling out of the tents, some of them only half-dressed. A second company of the 1/34th was ordered out to the *spur* to the north, and then a third.

The Zulu attack now developed with terrible rapidity. The *impi* came streaming down the slopes from the plateau along its whole length: and, as they advanced into the plain, the famous formation took shape. The Chest confronted the left centre of the camp. The Right Horn faced the camp's left flank and threatened to swing round the rear of Isandhlwana mount The Left Horn was attacking Durnford's *donga* and threatened to swing round towards Stony Hill and the *col*. It was reckoned

The 24th in Zululand

afterwards that more than 20,000 took part in the assault. 'The plain,' said a survivor, 'was black with Zulus.'

From front to rear the advancing host was at least a mile deep. Yet for all its unwieldy size, it moved with astonishing steadiness and precision. Silently, line on line, two or three yards between each man, it swept forward as smoothly as the incoming tide sweeps over the sand.

Durnford's little force had been the first to bear the full brunt of it; but the shelter of the *donga* enabled him to check it. 'All we could see were the helmets,' said one of the attacking Zulus afterwards. There is also on record a description of Durnford's conduct at this stage by a devoted Basuto who had been with him at Bushman's River Pass.

> The colonel rode up and down our line continually, encouraging us all—talking and laughing with us. "Fire, my boys! Well done, my boys!" he cried. Some of us did not like his exposing himself so much and wanted him to keep behind, but he laughed at us and said, "All right Nonsense . . . ."

The rifle fire was effective. The onrush was checked. Out in front of the *donga* dead Zulus lay thick. So heavy was the loss that presently, and before it had got near enough for flinging *assegais*, the frontal advance was halted and the Zulus lay down in the grass and waited, while, in accordance with the traditional tactics, the Left Horn continued its encircling movement. This could not be observed from the *donga*, but in any case, Durnford was now forced to retire for the simple reason that his ammunition was becoming exhausted. More than once he had sent back to the camp for more, but none had come.

As he withdrew, he was met by Essex, the letter-writer, who told him of the threat to his right and rear. Durnford must at once have realised its gravity. If the Zulus got round to the *col*, the only line of retreat for the whole force would be cut off. Most of his native troops seem now or a little later to have lost heart and slipped away, but, rallying his Colonial Horse and joined by a few more of them who had lost their bearings, Durnford withdrew to a position on the slope leading up to the *col*, determined to defend it to the last.

8

Meanwhile the main battle for the camp was being fought and lost.

Under pressure from the Right Horn and its encircling movement, the three companies of the 1/24th fell steadily back till they stood on a line running roughly east and west a few hundred yards from the left flank of the camp. Pulleine had hastily deployed the rest of his force to protect its front. The formation, naturally corresponding with the lay-out of the camp, was more or less rectangular. On the right of those three companies the line bent sharply southwards. In front of the corner and a little below it were Lonsdale's N.N.C. who had been posted, earlier on, along a small *donga* which branched at right angles from the big *donga* in the plain.

At the northern end of the line running south were the two guns which Chelmsford had not taken with him up the plain. When they first opened fire in the direction of the plateau, they were behind and a little above the N.N.C. A mistimed shell was seen to burst almost over their heads. Next the guns were the other two companies of the 1/24th; and somewhere near them those few Colonial Horse who had not ridden out with Chelmsford. Farther southward was the position to which Durnford was retiring on the slope up to the *col*; and on that slope or near it stood the one remaining company of the 2/24th.

It was not a bad defensive position. Except on the extreme left, the lie of the land was not unfavourable: the Zulus had to climb a slope. Boulders and smaller rocks provided a certain amount of cover. But there was one serious weakness. The line stretched at least 3,000 yards, and there were only 1,700 men—only 800 white men—to hold it. Nor was it an unbroken line. There were gaps of 200 yards or more between most sections of it. The gap to the north of Durnford's line of retreat was as much as 1,000 yards. If the troops had stood shoulder to shoulder—and that, as Chelmsford afterwards asserted, is what they would have done if only they had stayed within the camp—their resistance might have been prolonged.

Two other weaknesses—they proved disastrous—had nothing to do with the deployment of the white troops or the nature of the ground. First, the supply of ammunition was not organised. It did not matter so much that the line of battle was a few hundred yards away from the camp. Runners could have been posted to carry the precious cartridges when and where they were needed. But, since no heavy attack had been expected, this vital provision had been totally neglected. Many of the ammunition-boxes were still in the wagons or the mule-packs. From the boxes that had been unloaded the tight-screwed lids had not been taken off.

For the second weakness nobody was to blame. The corner of the rectangle was, of course, the most dangerous point of the defence; and by pure mischance it was precisely at that corner that, as the lines drew back, the N.N.C. fell into place. Save for the gallant Basutos out in the plain with Durnford, they were the only native section of the force. Most, if not all, of them had had no experience of battle; and they were mostly Zulus of a sort, Zulus who, though willing enough to take the field against their kinsfolk on the white man's side, had listened time and again to the story of what Chaka's and Dingaan's terrible warriors had done.

As the Zulu wave came surging forward, it was met with the same steady fire as at Durnford's *donga*. The Zulus were now meeting for the first time the volley-firing of British regulars. It made an unforgettable impression on them. It was 'terrible,' said a warrior who faced it. Terrifying also was the fire of the two guns, but only for a time. For the sharp-sighted Zulus learned quickly to observe the gunners 'standing clear' immediately before a gun was fired and promptly flung themselves to the ground. 'Only wind,' they shouted, as the shot whistled overhead and they sprang to their feet again. Thus, as a chief's son, cap-

Zulu Warriors

tured later, put it, 'the cannon did not do much damage. It only killed four men in our regiment: the shot went over us.'

For fifteen minutes or so the Zulu wave was held back by the volley-fire.

★★★★★★★★★★

There is a Zulu tradition that the front lines wavered and might even have retreated if they had not been rallied by a warrior who cried out with a great voice that Cetewayo had not ordered them to run away. (H. G. Lugg).

★★★★★★★★★★

Then, strengthened by other regiments from the rear, it rolled slowly on, till at last its foremost warriors came near enough to the N.N.C., who were a little in advance of the rest of the defence, to fling their *assegais*. Sixty yards more and they were ready to make their final charge. Up to that moment they had moved in utter silence. But now from end to end of their long front and from the ranks behind it, there rose a hoarse, ferocious, exultant cry like the roar of savage animals pouncing on their prey. At that dreadful sound the native levies blanched and fled. After them sprang the Zulus. In a moment they were through the yawning gap left open by the fugitives; and, since it lay at the corner of their rectangular position, the troops on either side of it were instantly outflanked. One of their officers wrote afterwards:

The five companies (of the 1/24th) were then together, firing volley after volley into dense masses of Zulus at only 150 yards range. The men were laughing and chatting and thought they were giving the blacks an awful hammering, when suddenly the enemy came down in irresistible numbers from the rear. The left and right flanks came in with a rush, and in a few minutes all was over.

A steady orderly retreat was utterly impossible. The ranks had been broken. White men and black men were entangled together. In a few minutes a confused fighting mob was surging back into the camp and eddying round the tents. Most of the natives bolted for the *col*. But there was no panic, no *sauve qui peut*, among the white troops. All the Zulus who were in the battle and spoke of it afterwards paid tribute to their bravery. One warrior recorded:

> Some Zulus threw *assegais* at them, others shot at them; but they did not get close—they avoided the bayonet; for any man who went up to stab a soldier was fixed through the throat or stomach and at once fell. Occasionally when a soldier was engaged with a Zulu in front another Zulu killed him from behind.

So the men of the 24th and the dismounted Colonial Horse, singly or in little groups, fought on. Some of them dived under wagons and fired from that poor cover. A quartermaster was stabbed as he was trying to unscrew an ammunition-box on the back of one of the mules that were galloping, mad with fright, among the combatants. Many brave deeds, no doubt, were done of which no record has survived; but one heroic incident was afterwards described by a British, and, more fully, by a Zulu witness of it, the latter said:

> He was a very tall man, and as we were rushing over the camp, he jumped on to an empty wagon with a gun and kept firing away, first on one side and then on another, so that no one got near him. We all saw him and watched him, for he was high up on the wagon, and we all said what a brave man that was. All those who tried to stab him were knocked over at once or bayoneted. He kept his ground for a very long time. Then someone shot him.

To fighting at such close quarters and against such overwhelming odds there could only be one end. Before long the Zulus had cleared the space between the tents in the northern part of the camp, and, rushing on to Chelmsford's headquarters, hauled down the flag that flew there and tore it to pieces. Meantime the surviving troops were trying to fight their way towards the *col*. To judge by the bodies and empty cartridges afterwards found there, Captain Younghusband and some sixty men of the 1/24th fell back right up to the foot of the mountain, and, there,

SKETCH OF THE BATTLE OF ISANDHLWANA.

on a rocky terrace, overlooking the *col*, they fought on till their ammunition was exhausted.

Of the rest some thirty succeeded in reaching the slope up to the *col*. A brave attempt was made to save the two guns. They were nearly lost on the first break-through. 'I saw one gunner stabbed,' reported a subaltern afterwards, 'as he was mounting on to an axle-tree box.' But the survivors managed to get them away, and, obstructed though they were by the rough rocky ground, to drive them up to the camp and through the *mêlée* within it. Almost all the gunners were now dead; but the horses were still alive and the guns actually reached the *col*, and, with fugitives clinging on to them like flies, were driven down the farther slope till they reached a gully that was quite impassable by anything on wheels. There they stuck. The drivers were torn from the horses and killed.

Meantime, on the slope below the *col*, Durnford was making his last stand. When threatened on his right as well as attacked in front, he had retired, as has been seen, as fast as possible in the hope of being able to keep open the one gateway of escape. But before he reached the crest of the *col* the tip of the Left Horn had swept up to Stony Hill, while the tip of the Right Horn had sped along behind the mount and was climbing the *col* from the rear. Durnford was thus almost completely surrounded. He can have had no hope; He had with him fifteen survivors of the Colonial Horse who, being mounted, could have made a bolt for safety but chose to abandon their horses and sell their lives at Durnford's side.

There were also those thirty odd survivors of the 1/24th. And close by—it is uncertain whether it actually joined up with Durnford's party—was the company of the 2/24th. Grouped in a rough square, the little band held the encircling Zulus for a time at bay; but at last, they were forced to yield their ground, step by step, till those that remained alive were standing back to back. When their ammunition was used up, the remnant fought on with their swords and bayonets till all of them were killed.

★★★★★★★★★★

A Zulu narrative of the battle describes this last stand.

'When we closed in, we came to a mixed party of mounted and infantrymen who had evidently been stopped by the end of our Horn. They numbered about a hundred. They made a desperate resistance, some firing with pistols and others using swords. I repeatedly heard the word "fire" given by someone. But we proved too many for them and killed them all where they stood. When all was over, I had a look at these men, and I saw an officer with his arm in a sling and with a big moustache, surrounded by *carabineers*, soldiers and other men that I didn't know.'

★★★★★★★★★★

It was now about 1.30 p.m.—only an hour and a half since the *impi* had begun to descend from the plateau. Below the great rampart of Isandhlwana the tents still stood in order and the wagons in their place. But of all the force which had moved about the camp, so free of care, that morning, not a man remained alive there. The few who had succeeded in breaking through the Zulus on the *col* were in headlong flight towards the frontier of Natal.

9

Many native fugitives had got away before the Zulus swept right through the camp. That anyone escaped after that was due to the fact that the Zulus had not completely occupied the *col*. One regiment was descending on it from the slope of Stony Hill; another, which had been sent round the back of the mount, was climbing up to it from the farther side. Thus, a narrow gap was left—perhaps for a few minutes only—and through it dashed the leaders of the rout, with a mob of mingled black men and white, of horse and foot, behind them. As the Zulus closed in, several others succeeded in cutting their way through. But the easy road to safety was barred. The Zulus were astride the track below.

The only chance was to make straight across the open country to the Buffalo; and down the rough stony slope the fugitives plunged. The Zulus were after them from the first, mixing with the crowd, stabbing the helpless foot-soldiers as they ran, keeping abreast of the horses, clutching hold of riders and dragging them from the saddle. One survivor told how 'a Zulu with a red feather' had seized his bridle. 'I tried to stab him with the bayonet, but he got hold of the rifle and pulled it out of my hands as if I had been a child.'

About half a mile from the *col* a deep steep-sided gully cut straight athwart the line of flight It was here that the guns were trapped. Fugitives on foot could scramble down one side and up the other; but it seemed afterwards hardly credible that several horses managed to get across. Brickhill, Pulleine's interpreter, who was one of the survivors, saw a 'Colonial' mounted on a 'noble grey' attempt to jump right over it. The horse fell far short of the farther bank and crashed with his rider to death below . . The scene at the gully is also described in a letter by Lieutenant Smith-Dorrien (afterwards General Sir Horace Smith-Dorrien), to his father. As they broke away from the camp, he wrote, they all made for the place where the Zulus seemed thinnest:

Everybody went pell-mell over ground covered with huge boulders and rocks until we got to a deep *spruit* or gully. How the horses got over I have no idea. I was riding a broken-kneed old crock which did not belong to me and which I expected to go on its head every minute. We had to go bang through them at the *spruit*. Lots of our men were killed there. I had lots of marvellous escapes, and was firing at them with my revolver as I galloped along.

Beyond the gully the ground was less open, covered with scrub, and cleft with ravines running down to the river. At times, says Smith-Dorrien, it was 'so broken that the Zulus went as fast as the horses and kept killing all the way.' At one point the fugitives found themselves on the edge of a steep precipice and had to dismount and lead their horses in single file. At another they were stumbling through a grass-covered bog. . . ,

Between the gully and the river, Brickhill caught up with Lieutenants Melvill and Coghill who had charged themselves with saving the colours of the 24th. 'Mr. Brickhill,' Melvill coolly asked, 'have you seen anything of my sword back there. .?' Another incident is reported by a Natal *carabineer*.

> As we were riding for our lives and the Zulus pursuing us, a trooper, named Kelly, staggered in his saddle, evidently hit by an *assegai* I stopped my horse to see what was the matter, and tried to support him but couldn't, and had to lift him off on to the ground. At that moment Dr. Shepherd came galloping past. (Surgeon-Major Peter Shepherd, M.B., Army Medical Department). I called out to him and he dismounted to examine poor Kelly. After carefully examining him, he said, "Poor fellow, too late, too late!" I had just mounted my horse and Dr. Shepherd was in the act of putting his foot in his stirrup when he was struck fatally by an *assegai*.

At last, they reached the Buffalo. Once across it, it was only twelve miles more, and better going, to Helpmakaar and safety. But the river was in spate. Swirling along its rocky bed, some 40 yards broad, it was quite unfordable, and its banks were very steep, in some places almost vertical. It was a disastrous check. The leading fugitives had begun to outdistance the pursuit, but now the exultant Zulus caught up with them, and many died who would have lived if the river had not held than back. Only some thirty white men got across, and for some of them it was almost a miracle. Smith-Dorrien wrote:

> We came to a kind of precipice, down to the River Buffalo. I jumped off and led my horse down. There was a poor fellow of the mounted infantry, a private, shot through the arm, who said as I passed him that if I would bind up his am and stop the bleeding, he would be all right. I accordingly took out my handkerchief and tied up his arm. Just as I had done it, Major ——— of the artillery came down by me wounded, saying, "For God's sake get on, man; the Zulus are on top of us." I had done all I could for the wounded man and so turned to jump on my horse.

Just as I was doing so, the horse went with a bound to the bottom of the precipice, being struck with an *assegai* I gave up all hope, as the Zulus were all round me, finishing off the wounded, the man I had helped and Major ———— among the number, However, with the strong hope that everybody clings to that some accident would turn up, I rushed off on foot and plunged into the river, which was little better than a roaring torrent I was being carried down the stream at a tremendous pace when a loose horse came by me and I got hold of his tail and he landed me safely on the other bank.

Brickhill also got ever. He says:

The river was rolling high, and there was no time for choosing a crossing place. My horse plunged in, swimming at once. . . . I clutched his mane and guided the rein with great care: yet four times I thought all was lost. Not ten yards below there was a waterfall in the pool of which three riderless horses were swirling round and round.

As he climbed the farther bank, Brickhill was fired on by Zulus from the other side. 'I saw a white man and a native fall off their horses here.'

What happened to Melvill and Coghill was learned from two or three survivors who got glimpses of them in or near the river. They reached the river together and plunged straight into it Melvill, 'encumbered by the colour, which is an awkward thing to carry even on foot,' found it difficult to keep his seat the saddle, and about half-way across he was swept away from his horse downstream, still clutching the colour. A little way down he bumped into a jutting rock to which a lieutenant of the N.N.C. who had also lost his horse was clinging. He too clung on and the lieutenant helped him to hold the colour. But the strength of the current soon swept both of them away downstream again.

Coghill, meantime had safely gained the farther bank. Looking back for Melvill and seeing him struggling with the colour in the river, he instantly plunged back into the stream. Almost at once his horse was shot dead, for the Zulus had now reached the river and were firing on the fugitives as they swam or climbed up the other side. So, Coghill was swirled away in Melvill's wake till they were both thrown up, not far apart, on the farther bank. The torrent had finally torn the colour from Melvill's grasp. It was afterwards found stranded lower downstream.

Melvill was quite exhausted. Coghill had not been weighed down by the colour, but had hurt his knee so badly that he could scarcely walk unaided. They managed to struggle some hundred yards up the steep hill, covered with rocks and thick bushes, that rose from the river bank; but they could get no further. They were last seen sitting down, revolver in hand, waiting for the Zulus who had crossed the stream. Their bodies were found there with several dead Zulus beside them. (Melvill and Coghill would have been recommended for the V.C. if they had survived—*Gazette*, May 2, 1879. It was posthumously awarded to them in 1907—*Gazette*, Jan. 15, 1907. They were buried side by side near where they fell).

The end of the story could not be better told than Smith-Dorrien tells it in that melodramatic, yet wholly unaffected, letter to his father. After losing his horse, he:

> . . . . ran on up a tremendous hill with my wet clothes and boots full of water. About 20 Zulus got over the water and followed us up the hill, but I am thankful to say they had not their firearms. . . . I was the only white man to be seen until I came to one who had been kicked by his horse and could not mount, I put him on his horse, and lent him my knife. He said he would catch me a horse. Directly he was up, he went clean away. A few Zulus followed us for about three miles across the river, but they had no guns, and I had a revolver, which I kept letting them know. . . .

★★★★★★★★★★

The pursuit seems to have been called off. Some Zulu *indunas*, who were afterwards asked whether, if they had captured Rorke's Drift, they would have invaded Natal, replied that 'they would not have exceeded the king's orders, which were that they were to resist to the utmost in Zululand, but not to invade Natal.'

★★★★★★★★★★

Well, to cut it short, I struggled into Helpmakaar . . . at nightfall, to find a few men who had escaped, about 10 or 20, with others who had been entrenched in a wagon-*laager*. We sat up all night, momentarily expecting attack. . . . We have not a single thing left. The men have no coats or anything, all being taken by the Zulus. We shall have another dreadful night of it tonight, I expect, lying on the wet ground. . . . Thank God I am alive and well, having a few bruises. God bless you.

So ends the young subaltern's remarkable letter. It must have taken his father's breath away.

10

It is time to return to Chelmsford and his column drawing near to Isandhlwana.

Night was falling as they marched, and, when about two miles from the camp they halted, it was quite dark. But the black outline of the mountain and Stony Hill and the *col* between than could be clearly seen against the starry sky; and on the *col* a few wagons were dimly visible. Some said they could see men moving about them. Others, more imaginative, thought they could faintly hear hoarse cries and the rattle of *assegais* on shields.

Were the wagons a Zulu barricade? In any case Chelmsford decided to attack the *col* forthwith. In view of that day's catastrophe, he had decided to retire the Central Column back across the frontier; and over the *col* ran the only track to the *drift* and the base at Helpmakaar. He ordered the guns to fire four rounds of shrapnel at the wagons on the crest

The sound of it broke the silence of the night, echoed against the mountain wall and round the hills about the plain, and, travelling on, was heard by Wood and his men sitting at their campfires twenty miles off. It died away and all was still again. Then the three companies of the 2/24th on the left flank were sent

113

on to take possession of Stony Hill at all costs, so as to command the *col* from above. They were to notify their capture of it by cheering. The rest of the force advanced a few hundred yards, then halted while another four rounds were fired at the *col*. Again, no answer but the echo. Nor was there any sound or sign of movement when, a little later, the 2/24th on the right were ordered to fire a volley in the hope of tempting the Zulus to betray their position.

As the men moved on again in the darkness, they presently began to stumble over dead bodies scattered here and there in the grass: a little further on they were lying thick. As they started to climb the slope leading up to the *col*, they heard a ringing cheer from Stony Hill. Since there had been no noise, there could have been no resistance; and, when they reached the crest, there was nobody behind the wagons. The whole site of the encampment, so full of life when they left it that morning, was deserted. They had been firing into the empty night.

It was now between 8 and 9 p.m. and Chelmsford decided to bivouac on the spot. So confident earlier in the day, he was now profoundly anxious. He could not gauge the full extent of the disaster, but the loss had obviously been heavy; and the victorious Zulu Army might still be close at hand. Weeks later it was known that, dismayed at the number of their best warriors killed in the battle—it was reckoned at about 3,900—they had retired that afternoon and dispersed to their *kraals*, taking the two cannon, some of the wagons, and all the ammunition and loot they could carry.

But Chelmsford could not know that. The silence might be a snare. The *impi* might be quietly waiting, somewhere in the darkness, to launch a sudden overwhelming attack. All night long, said one who was near him, he was pacing up and down behind the front ranks, 'watching and encouraging the men not to lie down and sleep.' But there was still no sign of Zulus. Watchfires were burning here and there in the distance, and at one point, in the direction of Rorke's Drift, the ominous glow of a bigger fire could be seen.

There were one or two false alarms, but nothing serious had happened when, in the dusk before dawn, Chelmsford ordered the column to fall in and continue its retirement. Such an early start was not unusual, but in this case, it was said to have been due to Chelmsford's fear lest his men's morale might be shaken by too clear a sight of the stricken field. As it was, their experience that night had been so gruesome, so macabre, as can rarely be equalled in all the annals of warfare. They had been on the march all day, and no reminders of the danger they were in could stop their lying down and trying to sleep.

As it happened, the site of the bivouac was where the dead lay thickest. On it or near it Durnford had made his last stand. Across it the mob of fugitives had fought to escape over the *col*. Many of the men, no doubt, fell asleep as soon as they lay down; but those who could not sleep found, as they moved their arms or turned from side to side, that they were touching the bodies of the dead, some of them their comrades of the morning.

The journalist, it will be remembered, had ridden out with Dartnell's force. In the course of the day, he had attached himself to Chelmsford's escort and he had spent the night beside his staff. An hour before daylight he nerved himself to visit the rite of the camp and he wrote a grisly account of what he saw there—white and black corpses mingled thick . . . most of the white men stripped to their shirts and boots, some mutilated, some headless. . . . dead horses, oxen, mules . . . wrecked wagons, boxes and sacks of stores lying broken open beside them, their contents—flour, biscuits, sugar, tea, oats, mealies—scattered about on the ground . . .

Another visitor to the desolate camp was Glyn. He recognised the bodies of Pulleine and Younghusband. Durnford's body was recognised by one of his men, stripped naked. Dead Zulus were lying 'in heaps.' Several loose wagon-wheels were scattered about; and round some of them, by a ghastly freak of fancy or savage ritual, the Zulus had laid out a circle of soldiers' heads.

As the troops set off on their march to Rorke's Drift—the

foot in column of fours, the horse in front and rear and presently thrown out on the flanks—they had to make their way through a jumble of derelict wagons on the crest of the *col*, pointing all ways, some jammed together, some overturned. Several oxen lay dead beside them, but others were 'alive in the yoke, standing there as if nothing had happened.'

For the first stage of the descent from the *col*, the low-lying country to the west and south was hidden from view by ridges of rising ground. The column, therefore, could not see the large body of Zulus which (as will presently be related) were bent on avoiding contact with them and hastily withdrawing north-wards. Nor could Rorke's Drift be seen till the head of the column climbed the rise and looked over the Bashee valley. Then all eyes were turned on the little mission-station across the river three or four miles away. It seemed as if the fears awakened by that big fire in the night had been justified. One of the buildings was still burning.

As they drew nearer, field-glasses revealed men moving about the station. It looked as if one of them was waving a flag. A detachment of horse was dispatched at full speed to cross the *drift* and find out quickly if indeed the garrison of the station had escaped the fate of the camp at Isandhlwana. As they galloped up the rise, they were greeted with a cheer.

11

While the battle was raging under the eastern wall of Isand-hlwana, a Zulu regiment, over 3,000 strong, had been sent round behind the mountain, at some distance to the north and west of it, to block the road to Rorke's Drift. If the stream of fugitives had been able to follow the road, still fewer would have escaped than the few that did. But, as has been seen, they had made, straight for the river; and the Zulus, too far north to observe the flight, decided to diverge from their course and attack Rorke's Drift itself. Cetewayo, it was learned later on from Zulu sources, had forbidden attacks on entrenched positions; and, since, as will appear, the position at Rorke's Drift was, however hastily and imperfectly, entrenched, the Zulu commander would have paid for his disobedience with his life if he had not been a member of the royal house.

The Oscarberg mission-station, which had been taken over from its Norwegian occupants to serve both as the base hospital and as a magazine for stores, stood on rising ground on the south or Natal side of the Buffalo. About 400 yards behind it was a rocky hill, its face broken by a ledge on to which one or two caves opened. Before it, 1,200 yards away, ran the river. The *drift* itself lay a little farther off to the left. Immediately in front of the buildings was a stretch of bush or scrub some thirty yards broad, then a road, and then a garden. The hill in the rear and the bush in front made it a weak position for defence.

Back to this spot came Lieutenant Chard, after parting from Durnford near Isandhlwana on the morning of the 22nd. Since his senior officer had gone to Helpmakaar to hasten up a company of the 24th which, had been ordered to reinforce the troops left to protect the *drift*, it fell to the subaltern to take command. His force that morning numbered about 200, half white, half black. The white force consisted of 98 men of the 2/24th, 11 of the 1/24th and 20 'odds and ends.' Twenty-eight of these were in hospital; so, the real white strength was almost exactly 100. The black force was a company of the N.N.C., which had been sent up earlier on from Helpmakaar, about 100 strong.

Chard, whose full and clear report supplies almost all our knowledge of the famous defence, was down at the '*ponts*' after lunch when, about 3.15 p.m., two horsemen came galloping down to the river and shouted to be taken over. One of them, a lieutenant of Lonsdale's N.N.C., told Chard of the disaster. The Zulus, he said, were on their way to the *drift*, and he stayed with Chard to help in its defence. The other horseman, a colonial *carabineer*, rode off to Helpmakaar to warn the base there to prepare for a Zulu attack. Ordering the tents by the river-crossing to be struck and their contents piled in a wagon.

Chard rode up to the station where he found a native messenger just arrived from Isandhlwana with the news that the

Zulus were advancing on the camp in force and with orders that he was to strengthen his position and hold it at all costs. Clearly not a moment was to be lost, and Chard (32 years) and his fellow subaltern, Lieutenant Bromhead, (34 years), set instantly to work, with the help of an officer of the commissariat named Dalton, to improve the defences of the station buildings.

Their lay-out was as follows. On the left stood the hospital, a single-storey building, facing towards the river, about 75 feet long by 36 broad. The interior was divided into several wards. About 30 yards to the east of it and 20 yards back towards the hill was the mission-house now converted into a store. Its dimensions were about 60 feet by 36. Close to its north-east corner stood a well-built stone cattle *kraal*, divided into two pens by a wall, and beyond it another larger, rougher *kraal*. Behind the hospital, about 12 yards off, ran a ditch with a two foot bank along it Behind the mission-house, some ten yards from its south-west corner, was a small cook-house and one or two open-air ovens. In the bare space in front of the mission-house lay by happy chance, a big heap of mealie bags. Happily too, a couple of wagons were standing nearby.

Directed by the subalterns and Dalton, the little garrison set to work, in desperate haste, to strengthen the defences as best they could. The windows of the hospital and mission-house were barricaded, and their walls pierced with loopholes; and all the way from a point some 20 feet in front of the north-west corner of the hospital to the small *kraal*—a distance of nearly 100 yards—a four-foot breastwork was built up with mealie-bags. A similar breastwork was built from the south-east corner of the hospital to the north-west corner of the mission-house, a distance of about 30 yards.

Into this the two wagons were fixed. While this work was going on, Chard rode down to the '*ponts*,' and brought up the sergeant and six men he had left there with the wagon. The sergeant and one of the men proposed that, if a few more men could be spared, they would moor the '*ponts*' in mid-stream and defend them from their decks. But, since he needed everyone who could hold a rifle at the station, Chard declined this plucky offer.

Chard had just got back to his post when an officer of Durnford's Basuto horse rode up. He had with him about 100 Basutos. Presumably they were the troop which Durnford had sent back before the battle to protect the wagons. They had halted somewhere on the track, one may suppose, waiting for further orders. If they saw the stream of fugitives to the south of them, it is to their credit that they did not also take to flight. Finally, they must have given up hope of their lost leader and ridden down to the *drift*. Their commander asked Chard for orders and was told to send some of his men to keep a close watch on the *drift* and others to look out for the Zulus, and, having done what they could to check their advance, to fall back on the station and help in its defence.

So strenuous, meantime, was the labour of the garrison that the breastworks of mealie-bags had been more or less completed when, about, 4.20 p.m., the first sound of firing was heard. It came from behind the hill, at the back of the station. The attack was coming, it seemed, not, as was to be expected, from the north across the Buffalo, but from the south. The Zulus, faithful to their customary technique of encirclement, must have crossed the river higher up and worked round to the back of the station.

At this critical moment Chard's force was seriously reduced. The officer in command of the Basutos came in to report that the Zulus were closing in and that his men refused to obey his orders to fall back on the station. Looking south-westwards Chard saw the whole body of horse riding off in the direction of Helpmakaar. A few minutes later the company of N.N.C. followed the Basutos' example and took the same road to safety. So, Chard was left with only the white half of his original garrison. It would be impossible, he saw at once, to hold the whole line of his defences if the Zulus were in strength. He would have to abandon the hospital and defend the mission-station only. So, he got his men, in still more feverish haste, to haul some big square wooden biscuit-boxes out of the store and to build a wall with them from the north-west corner of the house to the northern breastwork.

The wall was roughly four feet high when, about 4.30 p.m., the Zulus came in sight. Five or six hundred of them were seen moving round, the hill a quarter of a mile away; and in a moment they were making straight for the southern breastwork. Its defenders opened a steady fire on them, but they charged on till they were within fifty yards of it. There they came under cross-fire from the mission-house and were checked. Some of them took cover behind the cook-house and ovens and in the ditch and continued firing. But most of them, wheeling to their left, swept right round the hospital and attacked the north-west corner of the breastwork. Again, they were met by heavy fire and, after a desperate attempt to climb the mealie-bags, they were driven back into the neighbouring bush.

By now the main body had joined in the assault. A section of it climbed the ledge on the side of the hill. It overlooked the station, and, from such protection as the rocks and the mouths of the caves afforded, a steady fire was opened on the defenders of the breastworks and on anyone who ventured to cross the open ground between them. Meantime most of the main body, swerving again to the left round the hospital, occupied the garden and the road and the stretch of thick bush which, unfortunately, reached almost to the northern breastwork all the way along from the hospital to the line of biscuit boxes. Using it for cover, the swarming Zulus crept right up to the breastwork, and at one point after another along its length they tried fiercely to climb over it.

So close were they, and so furious was their courage, that sometimes they gripped with their bare hands the bayonets that held them off, and wrenched them from their sockets. They recked nothing of the twisted heaps of dead piling up against the breastwork. It gave them a foot-hold for getting at closer quarters with their *assegais*. But the third line of white men kept them at bay till, about sunset, the position was made untenable by the firing from the rear. More and more bullets were whistling down from the ledge on the hill behind the station, and, though they were not all well-aimed, the defenders of the northern breastwork had no protection against them and two or three were shot in the back.

Chard decided therefore that the time had come to evacuate the hospital and withdraw the whole garrison behind the wall of biscuit boxes.

Already for some time the Zulus had been trying to force their way through the barricaded doors and windows of the hospital. They had failed. There too their dead lay thick. But they had succeeded in throwing lighted brushwood on to the thatched roof and setting it on fire. Amid the sparks and smoke an heroic effort was made to bring out the inmates. The interior was defended ward by ward. While the patients were being helped out, two or three men kept the Zulus from the door. All the sick who were not too ill to walk were thus got safely away; and the rest might have been saved from their ghastly fate if doors had led from ward to ward.

As it was, holes were hacked in some of the mud-brick partitions with an axe. The last to leave the building were four privates of the 24th. Their ammunition exhausted, they held the main exit with the bayonet for a time till, seizing their chance, they ran back to the inner position.

During the evacuation of the hospital mealie-bags were heaped up in a rough circle a little to the west of the smaller, more solid *kraal* to form 'a sort of redoubt, which gave a second line of fire all round.' The first line was the adjacent strip of breastwork on one side are the mission house on the other. It was getting dark now, but the burning roof of the hospital gave light enough for aiming at the Zulus pressing in from north and west. Presently they seem to have broken into the mission-house: for Chard speaks of being completely surrounded at nightfall and being steadily forced back out of the redoubt and into the *kraal*. There they held for a time its western wall; and then fell back to the wall between the two pens. That last position they held to the end.

As night drew on, there was no lessening in the fury of the

attack. Again, and again the Zulus charged, recoiled, and after an interval charged once more. But for the burning hospital it would have been very dark—the new moon was only one day old—and the little garrison must have been overwhelmed by a surging mass of half-visible black men. But before long the fire had spread from the roof to the whole of the hospital building. All night long it burned, and in the light of the leaping flames the Zulus could be clearly seen, and the garrison, 'firing,' Chard reports, 'with the greatest coolness, did not waste a single shot. . .' It is a picture that will not easily fade—the flaming building, the charging savages, the *assegais* flashing in the lurid light, the white men and their two commanders shoulder to shoulder behind the stone wall of the *kraal*, firing steadily till the attackers melted away, watching for the next assault and firing steadily again.

After midnight the intervals between the attacks grew longer; the Zulus were beginning to weary of the slaughter. But it was not till about 4 a.m. that they finally lost heart. There were no more attacks after that. When dawn broke, an hour later, there was not a living Zulu to be seen. Round the station, thickest close beside its entrenchments, between three and four hundred lay dead. The casualties among the garrison, on the other hand, had been remarkably few. Only that gunfire from the ledge in the rear had had much effect.

Nor, seemingly, had flung *assegais* done much damage. As usual, the Zulus relied on getting to close quarters with the stabbing *assegai*; and, protected by the mealie-bags and the stone walls of the *kraal*, the defenders had been able to repel that assault with the bayonet without much loss. Thus the casualties were only fifteen dead (one of them a native) and twelve wounded, of whom two died. (Chard, Bromhead, Dalton and eight others were awarded the V.C. *Gazette*, May 2, June 17, November 18, December 2, 1880).

When daylight came, the survivors must have been near the point of physical exhaustion, and they could not be sure that another Zulu attack might not soon be launched, perhaps in still greater force.

About 7 a.m. it seemed as if indeed such a new attack was imminent. A large body of Zulus was sighted on rising ground to the north-east. Chard's report on this alarming development is as brief and calm as ever:

> I sent a friendly Kaffir, who had come in shortly before, to the officer commanding at Helpmakaar asking for help.

For a time, the Zulu force advanced towards the *drift*: then it halted and withdrew into the hills. The reason was soon evident. A long British column was marching down the track from Isandhlwana.

12

Of the handful of white men who escaped from Isandhlwana, a few stayed at Helpmakaar, the rest made for their homes deeper in Natal. Unnerved by their ghastly experience and physically exhausted, they carried panic with them as they rode. When the news reached Pietermaritzburg, it was not at first believed; but a statement signed by Frere and Bulwer soon made the bare facts known. Incredulity gave way to grief and consternation—grief at the loss of over a hundred young fellow-colonists who had ridden off so gaily to the war, consternation at the danger they were in themselves. The town was virtually defenceless. All the troops had marched off to join in the invasion. At any moment, it was thought, the triumphant Zulus might swoop down in overwhelming force.

The local volunteers were called to arms and new recruits enrolled. Defences were hurriedly improvised. Barricades of earth were built up round the Court House and its windows fitted with stout wooden shutters. War-correspondent Norris-

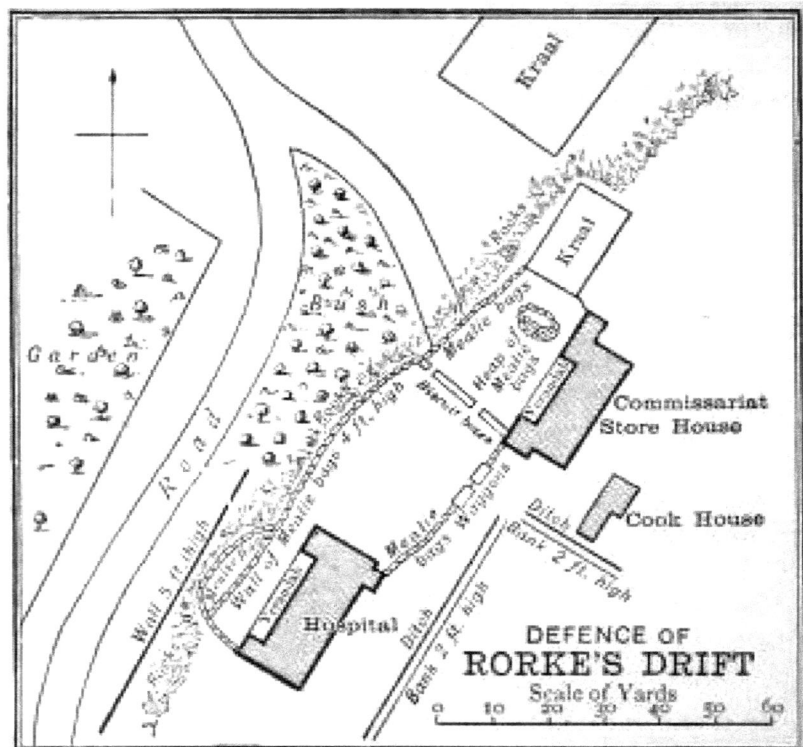

DEFENCE OF
RORKE'S DRIFT
Scale of Yards

Kraal

Kraal

Commissariat
Store House

Cook House

Garden

Road

Bush

Rocks

Mealie bags

Heap of
Mealie bags

Wall of Mealie bags 4 ft. high

Wall 5 ft. high

Wall of Mealie bags

Mealie bags Wagons

Ditch

Ditch
Bank 2 ft. high

Bank 2 ft. high

Hospital

0   10   20   30   40   50   60

Newman was one of the first to get back and he records how the people crowded round the post office on the chance of getting further news or stood in knots in the street, talking gloomily with lowered voices.

It was taken so much for granted that Cetewayo could have invaded Natal at that moment that various reasons were afterwards propounded as to why he did not. The general opinion has always been that his inaction was wholly due to the severity of the losses suffered at Isandhlwana and Rorke's Drift. But Colenso maintained that it was proof that he had not wanted war and was still ready to make peace. It might also have been argued that his strategy had always been defensive and that the sudden opportunity for invading Natal did not tempt him to depart from it. After all, he had expected his *impi* to wipe out the Central Column.

If he had intended a subsequent invasion, he would have ordered it beforehand. As it was, the pursuit beyond the Buffalo was soon called off; and the reason for that, according to Zulu prisoners captured later on, was, as recorded above, that Cetewayo had forbidden invasion. Another possibly explanation was found in the fact that the Tugela was in flood, an unusually high flood. It had always been regarded by the Zulus as setting a limit to campaigning in the rainy season: 'the Tugela,' went the saying, 'is a greater chief than the Zulu king.' And in this particular season it would have been very difficult for a host of unmounted Zulus to cross it. But none of these explanations are really needed.

If Cetewayo had wanted to fling an *impi* over the border, he could not have done it for the simple reason that there was no *impi*. The spirit of the regiments which fought at Isandhlwana and Rorke's Drift had not been broken by their losses, but for the moment they had had enough of British rifle-fire, and, having 'washed their spears,' had dispersed to their homes with their booty, not on orders from Ulundi, but by a natural impulse often paralleled in the annals of native warfare. It was several weeks before the regiments could be re-assembled.

Unaware of this, Chelmsford for his part had decided to hold up the whole campaign and withdraw his base right back to Pietermaritzburg. He arrived there on the morning of January 26, 'looking many years older,' noted Frere, 'so changed and worn by anxiety and sleeplessness,' Next day he dispatched his first report on the disaster to the Secretary of State for War (F. A. Stanley). It was a provisional report, pending the outcome of a Court of Enquiry which 'will, I trust, be able to collect sufficient evidence to explain what at present appears to me almost incomprehensible.'

He had left a substantial force in the camp with orders to defend it If it had 'taken up a defensive position in the camp itself, and utilised there the materials for a hasty entrenchment which lay ready to hand, I feel absolutely confident that the whole Zulu Army would not have been able to dislodge them.'

The Court of Inquiry had assembled that same day at Helpmakaar. Colonel Hassard, R.E., presided: the other two members were Colonels Law and Harness. Evidence was taken from eight witnesses—Clery, Glyn, Gardner, Essex, Cochrane, Smith-Dorrien, Nourse and Curling. Only Gardner, Essex, Cochrane, Nourse and Curling (the last a lieutenant with the guns) had anything to say about the battle itself. They agreed that Durnford had taken his force out some miles from the camp. And it was this point that became the mainstay of Chelmsford's defence.

Since Durnford had been in command, it had been assumed from the outset that the responsibility for what happened had been mainly his. It had been spoken of as 'poor Durnford's defeat' And now the theory gained ground that all would have been well if Durnford, ignoring the order to defend the camp, had not gone so far afield with his own troops and drawn out Pulleine's troops to his support, so that the battle was fought in open order at a distance from the camp instead of in close order within it. Pearson, in a message from Eshowe, put it in everyday language:

How very foolish of poor Durnford's detachment to scatter about so far from the camp!

More formally expressed, this theory was the basis of Chelmsford's *apologia* in subsequent dispatches and in the speech, he made in the House of Lords on his return to England. That speech was characteristically simple, forthright and generous. He firmly rebutted the suggestion that the troops at Isandhlwana were of poor quality, not seasoned and disciplined enough to face a crisis without wavering. 'Two finer battalions,' he said of the 14th, 'could not have been found.' Nor did he omit to pay a tribute to the 'gallantry and steadiness' of the Basutos. The account he gave of the battle—the 'true, plain, unvarnished tale,' he called it—was, with one exception to be mentioned presently, in accordance with the facts as far as they could be ascertained without evidence from the dead. But there was less certainty in the inference he drew from them.

> The camp was not lost through having an insufficient garrison, or because the position was an unfit one for the number of troops to defend, but because the strict orders for the defence which had been given were not carried out.

Chelmsford believed that; and his honesty is unquestionable. Yet it was only half the truth—and the less decisive half.

On the morrow of the disaster Chelmsford was denounced in the press, both in Natal and in England, as its sole author; and it was not unnatural that the members of his staff, who must be taken to have shared in some degree their chief's responsibility, should be up in arms in his defence. It was natural, too, that Chelmsford's many friends should welcome an explanation which made him appear the victim somebody else's mistakes. But the defence was overdone. If it was unjust to hold Chelmsford solely responsible, it was no less unjust to shift the sole responsibility on to Durnford. And the attempt to do so involved some serious aberrations.

The first was a *suggestio falsi*. It was, intimated, though never plainly stated, that Pulleine was ordered in precise unmistakable terms that he was not on any account to move any of his troops (save outposts, of course) beyond the perimeter of the camp while the main force was away. What were the orders? They were actually given by Glyn as commander of the column and conveyed to Pulleine both in writing and by word of mouth by Major Clery, Glyn's staff officer. Since no copy of the written orders survived. Clery could only recite them from memory.

> Draw in your camp or your line of defence (I am not certain which) while the force is out: also draw in the line of your infantry outposts accordingly, but keep your cavalry vedettes still for advanced.

Clearly this forbade such a dispersal of the troops as did in fact occur: but if the danger of a Zulu attack in such great strength as to require defence in close order within the camp had been foreseen, surely Pulleine would have been given quite explicit instructions to that effect. Such a danger, of course, was not foreseen.

Next came the charge—and this was the one dubious statement of fact in Chelmsford's speech—that Durnford was responsible for all the movements outside the camp. He had not only taken his own force down to the plain. He had also ordered that first company of the 1/24th to go out to the northward *spur*. There is no reliable evidence as to who gave that order, (See Note B), but it seems in the highest degree improbable that Durnford gave it. The position on the *spur* was nearly a mile and a half from the camp. Is it not reasonably certain that Pulleine would have objected to sending out that one company to that distance as firmly as he objected to sending out the two companies with Durnford? If he did object, is it likely that Durnford overrode him in that case when he refused to do so in the other?

And why, finally, if the question was discussed, did the staff officer who heard and recorded the lunch-time conversation in Pulleine's tent, say nothing about it? Surely it was Pulleine who sent the company to the ridge, after Durnford had gone. Left in command, he was plainly entitled to do so, and is it not probable that he did it because he became anxious as to the safety of his northern flank?

The next charge against Durnford seems even less tenable. It was argued that the further extension of Pulleine's troops outside the camp was Durnford's fault because they were sent out to support him when he got into difficulties. Was not that precisely what he had asked Pulleine to do before he left? But in fact, the second and third companies of the 1/24th were not sent out to support Durnford, but to support the first company on the ridge when it found, itself confronted with the *impi* advancing over the plateau. Durnford, it is true, was also confronted by the Zulus at about the same time. But he was at least two miles away to the east. The companies sent to the *spur* had nothing to do with him. His battle out on the plain was remote and distinct from the battle on the *spur*.

The same applies to the subsequent movement of the fourth and fifth companies of the 1/24th and of the guns. Pulleine hastily threw them forward, not, of course, to support Durnford, retreating well away in the plain, but to support the right flank of the first three companies and to meet the Zulu threat to the north-east section of the camp. Nor did Durnford really need support. He was not in serious danger at that time. Except for the rocket-battery and its escort, all his force was mounted. If he had chosen, he could safely have retreated faster than he did. As it was, the main battle had been lost and the camp was being overrun before he got back to the *col*.

There was one more accusation, and this so flimsy as to be almost ludicrous. It was stated at the time, and the statement has been repeated in recent years, that the Zulus would not have attacked the camp on the fatal day if Durnford's Basutos had not drawn them on. That, no doubt, is true; but only of that day. For, suppose the Zulus had been left alone, suppose Durnford had kept his force in camp, what would have happened? The *impi* would have remained in hiding waiting for the attack planned for the early hours of the morrow. Their presence was not detected between dawn and noon. Presumably it would have remained undetected between noon and sunset.

About 4 p.m. Chelmsford and his staff would have ridden in. He would have dined, and gone to bed in his headquarters with the same sense of security as on the two previous nights.

★★★★★★★★★★

Since the force at the camp would have been smaller, Chelmsford might possibly have attempted same entrenchment; but these would not have been much time for it before dark, and, in view of his conviction that there could be no large body of Zulus in the neighbourhood, it seems unlikely that he would have, troubled about it.

★★★★★★★★★★

In the dusk before the dawn the Zulus would have launched their attack. There would have been no time for organised resistance. The camp would have been overwhelmed even more quickly and completely than it was. The survivors would probably have been even fewer. Certainly, Chelmsford would not have tried to escape. It may be said, indeed, that, if the Basutos had not stirred up the Zulus, the catastrophe would still have occurred, and it would have been even more disastrous than in fact it was.

In any case to narrow the issue to the question of responsibility for the disobeying of the orders is to evade a more decisive question. It is tacitly assumed that, if the orders had been obeyed, the Battle of Isandhlwana would have ended in as complete a repulse of the Zulus as the defence of Rorke's Drift. But is that an unchallengeable assumption? It must be remembered, first, that if all the troops had been kept within the camp, the line they would have had to defend would still have been long. It would have had to stretch from the north end of the mountain round the tents and below the *col* to the south end of Stony Hill, a distance of about 1,800 yards.

And troops would also have been needed to protect the western side of the *col* from attack round the rear of the mount and to occupy also the crest of Stony Hill, since it commanded the *col*, and also, surely, the summit of the mount itself, since it was not by any means impossible for a dangerous number of Zulus to climb its western face.

For all these purposes the troops available numbered 800 whites and 900 blacks. That would certainly have made possible a defence in relatively close order; but to infer from that that it would have been as successful a defence as that of Rorke's Drift is to ignore the vital point of difference between them. Part of the garrison at the *drift* was protected in the first stage of the assault by the walls of houses. In the later stages all of it was protected either by the barricade of mealie-bags or by the stone walls of the *kraal*. There was no such protection at Isandhlwana. There was no entrenchment; and, whatever defences might have been hastily improvised when the advance of the *impi* was detected, a breast-high barricade could certainly not have been built in the time allowed.

Thus, the troops would have been exposed not only to flung *assegais* but also to rifle-fire, of which some would have been erratic, but some, as at Rorke's Drift, would have told. And, that being so, is it probable that the defenders of the camp, outnumbered by more than ten to one—if the natives had fled, by more than twenty to one—could have held their ground to the end? They would have held it longer, no doubt, than, in the actual event they did. But could they have held it long enough for Chelmsford to discover what was really happening and come to their rescue in time?

There seems ground for the opinion, therefore, that obedience to orders would not have prevented the disaster, because an order to entrench the camp before the fatal day was never given. The reason for this omission was stated on an earlier page, but it may be restated here, for therein lies the root of the whole matter. The precautions, which seemed so manifestly needed after the event, were not taken before it because neither Chelmsford nor any of his officers were aware that a huge *impi* of Zulus could move across country at no great distance from them without being seen. They took it for granted, as has more than once been pointed out, that no large force of Zulus could be near Isandhlwana at the time the camp was pitched or on the two following days.

If that had been true, it may be argued, no mistakes were made. It was safe to leave the camp unfortified. It was safe for Chelmsford to sleep there two nights and intend to sleep a third. It was safe for him to take most of the column away. It was safe for Durnford to ride out into the plain and for Pulleine to send his men up to the *spur*. In none of these cases would the presence of small Zulu forces in the neighbourhood have been a serious danger; but if an *impi* could approach as near as it did on that disastrous day and remain concealed, then, in all of those cases, a terrible risk was run.

Thus, the issue resolves itself into a single and simple question. Could Chelmsford or his senior officers be blamed for not realising how secretly great masses of Zulus could move? Surprise, it is true, was the traditional objective of Zulu strategy; and Kruger had warned Chelmsford against it. But Kruger did not tell him—it may be doubted, indeed, if he knew himself—with how huge a force surprise could be achieved.

And how, in fine, it may be asked, could Chelmsford acquire this knowledge except by experience, in his case harsh experience? If he can be blamed—as perhaps he may—for being so confident of his security in face of an enemy whose military power and technique were not yet fully known to him, beside him in the pillory must stand those more distinguished generals who, twenty years later, made the same mistake when they first confronted the Boers and at far greater loss of British lives than was suffered at Isandhlwana.

Sequel

1

Unfortunate in the calamity that befell him at the outset of the war, Chelmsford was fortunate in being able to retrieve it. Most defeated generals have been superseded on the morrow of their defeats; but, more than five months after Isandhlwana, Chelmsford was in command at Ulundi and by a decisive victory brought the war to an end.

He had asked to be relieved of his charge in a telegram to the War Office in February, but no action was then taken. The government had been shaken by Isandhlwana—it was one of the reasons for their defeat at the elections in the spring of 1880—and Disraeli in particular had taken it hard. He confided to Lady Bradford:

> I am greatly stricken. Everybody was congratulating me on being the most fortunate of ministers when there comes this horrible disaster.

Nor could there be any quick escape from the entanglement in Zululand. The war had to be seen through; and the government, accepting Chelmsford's version of the catastrophe, backed as it was by Frere, decided to keep him for the time being at his post. Reinforcements, so reluctantly conceded before, were now provided speedily and without stint. By May Chelmsford found himself in command of at least thrice as many white troops as those with which he had first invaded Zululand; but mainly owing to the extreme difficulty of obtaining wagons and their teams and enlisting natives, all terrified by Isandhlwana, to drive them, it was not till the beginning of June that the second invasion began.

Meantime the original Right and Left Columns had both been in action. On April 3, Chelmsford had relieved the Right Column besieged at Eshowe and withdrawn it to the frontier without heavy fighting. It was against the Left Column that the reassembled Zulus directed their main force. On March 12 a British convoy, bringing up supplies from the rear, was caught at the Intombe River and more than half wiped out. On March 28 Wood ordered his mounted troops to scale Zhlobane Mountain. It was a blunder. The stony, steep ascent was difficult for horses, and when the troopers had reached the plateau on the summit, they were nearly surrounded by an *impi* rapidly approaching from the south.

In the desperate retreat nearly a hundred officers and men were killed, including the veteran Boer frontiersman, Piet Uys. (For his courage in this action Major Redvers Buller was awarded the V.C.) Next day the *impi* fell on the camp at Kambula to which Wood had withdrawn. He had not, it seems, expected an, immediate attack, and only the chance warning of a friendly native enabled him to strengthen his defences in time. Beside the small redoubt which had previously been built and a stone cattle *kraal*—quite insufficient by themselves to protect a force of about 2,000—a roomy and close-knit wagon-*laager* was formed. The hardest-fought action of the war ensued.

The Zulus were in great strength. Their *impi* included some of the regiments which had triumphed at Isandhlwana. For four hours they continued, with their usual disregard of death, to press their assault. The *kraal* was lost. One side of the *laager* was seriously menaced. An eye-witness said:

> For a long time, it was touch and go till at last a shiver seemed to run through the enemy and all in a moment they broke and fled.

At length, on June 1, the second invasion began. But by then

PIET UYS

the government in far-away London had lost patience. Why this interminable delay? asked the Opposition: and the question was echoed in the press, Disraeli had no confidence in Chelmsford's capacity to handle the large force he now commanded, and after several weeks' discussion it was decided to send out to supersede him a soldier who had an unbroken record of success in native warfare and who, if he did not know Zululand, at any rate knew Natal. On May 28 a telegram was dispatched from the War Office informing Chelmsford that Sir Garnet Wolseley was coming out with plenary civil and military powers in South-East Africa, and, while deprecating the notion that any censure of Chelmsford was involved, directing him to subordinate his plans to Wolseley's control.

Long before he could receive this message of recall—as in fact it was and as Disraeli afterwards admitted it had been—Chelmsford was cautiously advancing into Zululand. He had learned his lesson. All the precautions neglected before were taken now. Among his detailed instructions were the following:

> Companies must be kept together in close order. Files may loosen out but will not be extended. . . . The force will form a square *laager* of the wagons every night with a shelter trench round it, 9 ft from the wagons. . . . Each wagon and cart with the convoys must have some ammunition boxes placed on it in such a position as to be easily got at . . . Each wagon or cart will have a screwdriver attached to one of the boxes. . . .

This time the invasion was to be conducted by two main forces. The first or southern division, 9,200 strong, under H. H. Crealock, (Major-General. Brother of Lieut.-Colonel J. N. Crealock, Chelmsford's military secretary), moved along the coast and occupied Port Durnford, a secondary base of supply, without meeting any opposition. The second or northern division, 9,000 strong, under Newdigate, moved eastwards from Dundee across the Buffalo and made more or less straight for Ulundi 70 odd miles away. To it were attached a cavalry brigade of 1,270 under Marshall and a 'flying column' of 3,000 under Wood. Chelmsford accompanied it in supreme command.

As fate willed it, the second invasion suffered like the first a stroke of misfortune at the outset, very different in its character and scope, but equally resounding. Against the wish of the British Government, the young Prince Imperial, only son of the widowed Empress Eugenie, who had made her home in England after the *débâcle* of 1870, had accompanied the reinforcements dispatched to Natal at the beginning of the year. He was attached to the second division, and on June 1, while the division was marching to its first night's camping ground near Itelezi Hill, he rode out in advance of it on patrol. With him went a lieutenant of the 98th regiment, six troopers of Colonial Horse and a native guide. Their task was to reconnoitre the route which the division was to take next day—a preliminary reconnaissance had found the neighbourhood quite empty of Zulus—and to choose a site for the night's encampment.

About 2.30 they reached a native *kraal* near the junction of the Ityotysi and Tombokala Rivers. The huts were deserted. There was not a Zulu to be seen. Off-saddling and tethering their horses, they sat down to make some coffee and rest. After an hour or more of peace and quiet they had begun to saddle up for the ride back to camp, when suddenly there came a burst of rifle-fire from the long grass growing only some fifteen yards away. No one was hit, but the horses were startled, the prince's horse so violently that, athlete though he was, he could not mount it. The rest of the party had got some distance away before they discovered that the prince was not with them.

He was lying dead, his body gashed with many *assegai* wounds. . . . The sense of complete security, the belief that there were no Zulus about, their undetected presence so very near—it was Isandhlwana in miniature. And, though the loss of life was so immeasurably less, such was disposition of the prince, the attractiveness of his gallant personality and the romance which clung to it, that the news of his death stirred the emotions of the public in England and on the Continent as deeply as the news of Isandhlwana.

The advance was slow. . .'Perverse pedestrianism,' it was called by Archibald Forbes, the *Daily News* correspondent, in a sardonic article published in the following spring. But at any rate this time it was sure. As each cautious step was taken, the surrounding country was scoured by strong mounted patrols. If no large Zulu forces were discovered, it was because they were not there. In the course of the advance several messages came in from Cetewayo asking for terms of peace; but to the stiff conditions laid down by Chelmsford there was no response. At last, on July 1, the British column reached the Umvolosi River at a point some five miles from Ulundi. On the farther side of the river towards Ulundi all that remained of Cetewayo's military machine, an *impi* numbering upwards of 20,000, was gathered for the last battle of the war.

Early on July 4, the British troops quietly crossed the river, covered by a mounted force, and advanced in a hollow 'square'—in fact an oblong—towards Ulundi. The flanks were manned by British regulars, 12 companies in each of the longer lines, 5 companies in the front line, 4 in the rear. Six 9-pounder guns, six 7-pounders and two Gatlings were disposed, at intervals. The native contingent, numbering 958 strong, marched within the square. Into it also the cavalry were withdrawn when, about 9 a.m., the Zulus attacked on all sides.

The frenzy of their assault was as fierce as ever; but they had never met such concentrated gun and rifle-fire and only at one point, where the lie of the ground was favourable, could they get near enough to fling their *assegais*. It was all over in half an hour. About 9.30 the attack began to weaken and waver, and when the cavalry were launched from within the square, the whole *impi* broke and fled. The Zulu losses can only be guessed at—perhaps 1,500 killed. The British casualties were 12 killed and 88 wounded.

Ulundi was found deserted. Cetewayo had taken refuge in the depths of the Ngome Forest, 30 miles or so away to the north. Having burnt the royal *kraal* and all the military barracks in its neighbourhood, Chelmsford—needlessly, it was afterwards suggested—withdrew his troops southwards.

He had only just had time to retrieve his reputation. The official announcement of Wolseley's appointment had been more than, usually delayed; but Reuter's version of it reached Capetown on June 14. Frere promptly telegraphed the unexpected news to Chelmsford and followed it up with a sympathetic letter:

I cannot tell you how glad I am to hear of your being able to move on and how confidently I hope that you will have a brilliant success before anyone comes to share the fruits of all your labours, trials and sufferings.

On June 23 Wolseley reached Capetown and at once assumed command of all the British forces in South Africa. On June 30, he telegraphed his general instructions to Chelmsford: they reached him two days before the battle. By that time Chelmsford had decided to resign. On July 15 he met Wolseley at St. Paul's mission-station. On the 26th he sailed for home from Durban.

He was well received in England. Ulundi had wiped out Isandhlwana in the public mind; and, impersonating it as she so often did, the queen summoned him without delay to Balmoral. In due course he was awarded the G.C.B., a high distinction for a soldier of his rank. Only Disraeli, it seemed, could not forgive the man whom he held responsible first for backing Frere in bringing about the war and then for its disastrous opening and subsequent prolongation. It had cost over 1,000 British lives and over 5,000,000 British pounds. It had embarrassed his international diplomacy at a critical time. It had undermined his government's prestige. No: he would not accept the queen's suggestion that he should invite the man to Hughenden.

2

Frere was less fortunate than Chelmsford. He could not win a Ulundi. So Isandhlwana broke him.

Almost at once the critics of the government in England shifted from the question of responsibility for the disaster to the prior and greater question of responsibility for the war. Three days after the news reached London, the *Daily News*, the chief Liberal organ, declared that 'the war was entirely of our own seeking.' A few weeks later a full-dress attack was launched in Parliament. On March 25 a motion was brought forward in the Lords, censuring Frere's policy and regretting that he had not been recalled. It was a poor debate, The most pointed sentence spoken in it was Carnarvon's:

> But for the unfortunate disaster at Isandula, I do not believe he (Frere) would have stood in need of defence here tonight.

Since the motion was virtually a vote of censure, the division was on purely party lines—156 to 61 against. The proceedings in the Commons, where the same motion was introduced by Dilke on March 97, were livelier.

'Ability misdirected,' said Joseph Chamberlain, 'is more fatal than ignorance itself"; and he charged the government with infecting the minds of their agents overseas with their 'new imperialism.' Harcourt was at his best and most satirical. He recited an imaginary letter from the Secretary of State to Frere.

> Dear Sir Bartle Frere. I cannot think you are right. Indeed, I think you were very wrong; but after all I feel you know a great deal better than I do. I hope you won't do what you are going to do; but, if you do, I hope it will turn out well.

The motion was lost by 306 to 246.

The government's position was unquestionably weak. If they had told Frere plainly, and before it was too late, that there must be no war, then they could honestly have put all the blame on him and immediately recalled him. But that course was ruled out, and it was decided that Frere as well as Chelmsford should be retained, at least for the time being. When Hicks Beach received the text of the fatal ultimatum on January 2, he had realised what it meant, but he had not written to Frere about it till

January 23, the day on which the Central Column was marching back from Isandhlwana and panic was spreading through Natal.

As was natural enough in the circumstances, it had been a hedging letter. He regretted 'that the necessity for immediate action should have appeared to you so imperative' as to preclude the delay required for submitting the ultimatum for approval in London. But he did not wish 'to question the propriety of the policy adopted'; and he sincerely hoped that it would prove successful, and that:

> If military operations should become necessary, the arrangements' which you have reported may secure that they should be brought to an early and decisive termination with the result of finally relieving Her Majesty's subjects in Natal and the Transvaal from the danger to which they are exposed.

How clear that makes it that Frere would have emerged from the crisis with heightened prestige, that his 'insubordination' would have been forgotten, if Isandhlwana had not happened. But it did happen, and, confronted with the storm it raised in press and Parliament, the government, naturally again, took a firmer line with Frere. But it was still only a half-measure. He was sharply reprimanded, but not recalled. In a dispatch, not sent off till March 13, Hicks Beach told Frere that the government were not convinced by the evidence he had supplied of the 'urgent necessity for immediate action which alone could justify you in taking, without their full knowledge and sanction, a course almost certain to result in a war.'

But they recognised the 'unusual powers' which had been entrusted to him and highly appreciated the energy and ability with which he had exercised them. Since, therefore, he was unlikely to repeat his mistake, they had 'no desire to withdraw, in the present crisis of affairs, the confidence hitherto reposed in you, the continuance of which is now more than ever needed to conduct our difficulties in South Africa to a successful termination.'

What was Frere to make of this two-sided document? He

must have asked himself whether open censure—for the dispatch was published—would not so discredit him as to cripple his capacity to carry on. But the government's appeal to him to stay seemed genuine enough, and it was backed from many other quarters. Carnarvon wrote:

> Consider well, before you resign. . . . Your resignation at this juncture would invoke grave embarrassment—perhaps even disaster.

Morier, soon to be regarded as one of the shrewdest of British diplomats, wrote:

> Hold on, till you have finished your work.

It was clear, too, that Frere had lost no credit with British colonial opinion. It had warmly backed him against the Zulus. It backed him no less warmly now against ignorant critics in England. Meetings were held, addresses carried by acclamation, in every town of any size. Gordon Sprigg, Prime Minister of Cape Colony wrote:

> If you were now to retire, the consequences to South Africa would be simply disastrous.

All this must have reinforced Frere's inward longing to stay. He believed himself better seized of the realities of the situation in South Africa than anyone else, and there might be a chance, after all, that he would be able to 'finish his work.' So, he stayed. He defended himself against the censure in a long dispatch. He admitted no mistake: he reiterated his case that the delay of several months required for submitting the ultimatum for approval would have precipitated a catastrophe. Ministers, indeed, may well have been nettled by this cool self-confidence; and Disraeli for one was as angry with Frere as with Chelmsford. He blurted out to Lady Chesterfield:

> Sir Battle Frere, who ought to be impeached, writes always as if he were unconscious of having done anything wrong.

But so he was, and therefore the weight of the next blow that fell on him was all the heavier.

It has already been recorded that, as the Zulu war dragged on, the government decided to send out Wolseley to supersede not only Chelmsford in the field of war but also Frere in the whole area surrounding it, and that the contents of the dispatch embodying this decision, becoming known to Reuters, were telegraphed to the Cape some weeks in advance of the dispatch itself. So Frere did not know of Wolseley's appointment before it appeared in the local newspapers.

This was a very much, more serious matter than the reprimand. The whole control of policy in Natal, the Transvaal and Zululand was taken out of his hands. The forwarding of federation, it was argued, was his primary task, and this now required his presence at the Cape a thousand miles away from the area which had become so critical It was to be only a temporary limitation of the High Commissioner's authority, and it was assumed that Frere would acquiesce in it. But was that a genuine assumption? Surely it was obvious that his superiors in London no longer cared whether he stayed on at the Cape or not.

Yet he did stay on, for much the same reason, no doubt, as before, though this time it is more difficult to understand his decision. He stayed on to see the situation growing worse and quite unable to prevent it. There was no difficulty at Capetown. The tide there had begun to flow in favour of federation. But it was soon checked by the trouble in the north—in the Transvaal and in Zululand. And in both the Transvaal and Zululand the plans Frere had conceived were set aside. He had intended to take a strong line in Zululand and a conciliatory line in the Transvaal. The policy which Wolseley brought out with him, after consultation with Hicks Beech and other ministers, was exactly the opposite.

Frere had appreciated—though by no means sufficiently—the strength of Boer patriotism in the Transvaal. He had met Kruger and his comrades and liked them. He wrote home:

They deserve respect and regard, for many valuable and

amiable qualities and felt very deeply what they believed to be a great rational wrong (*i.e.*, the annexation).

He realises that a Boer rebellion was not by any means impossible and that the only way to forestall it was to concede at least a modest measure of self-government. He proposed that the executive council should be expanded for legislative purposes into a legislative council in which five officials would be outnumbered by nine nominated non-officials. At the end of eighteen months the possibility of elected members, in other words representative government of a sort, would be considered in the light of experience. That was not nearly enough, but it was something.

The constitution proclaimed by Wolseley in September provided for an executive council only, composed of five officials against three nominated non-officials. There was no suggestion of representative government and Wolseley declared open war on the 'patriots.' He told a public meeting at Pretoria in December:

The agitators, are the greatest enemies of this country and its institutions.

It was they who had made the grant of representative government impossible. He said a few months later:

The aggravation of such tumours in a body politic must be arrested.

Only the townsmen in the Transvaal, mainly British, cheered these sentiments. More and more of the Boer farmers began sullenly to side with the 'agitators,' demanding the undoing of the annexation and the restoration of the free Republic.

Frere had recommended the annexation of Zululand. He believed that, like the parts of Kaffraria already annexed to Cape Colony, it could be easily administered by British magistrates, that the Zulus would prove amenable to civilising influences, and that a moderate hut-tax would pay the cost not only of current government but even of the war itself.

Wolseley's policy, on the other hand, was the complete withdrawal of British authority. The Zulus were to be left to themselves again. But with this difference: they would have no great king. The country was divided into thirteen sections under thirteen little 'kings.' There was to be a British Resident to serve as 'the eyes and ears' of the British Government, but he would have no authority of his own. ('Where', was Frere's caustic question, 'are his arms and legs?') This settlement soon proved the failure it was bound to be. Before long the little kings were fighting among themselves, and by 1882 it was admitted that no stability was possible in Zululand without 'a duly recognised and adequate authority.'

But the Government was still averse from annexation. Since the vacant place was not to be filled by a British official and since there was nobody else to be found, they decided to reinstate Cetewayo, who had been captured soon after Ulundi and smuggled away to the Cape where he was still living in detention. He was brought to England, received by the queen at Osborne, and lectured on the principles of good government by Kimberley. He was to rule only over Central Zululand, but ever that diminished power he could not exercise for long.

The chiefs had tasted freedom, and their sometime overlord had been discredited by defeat and captivity. Within six months he was a fugitive. Within thirteen months he was dead. In 1884 the British flag was hoisted at St Lucia Bay just in time to forestall its occupation by the Germans. In 1887 the rest of Zululand was proclaimed British territory in order to forestall its occupation by the Boers. At last, in 1897, it was annexed to Natal.

Only the first chapter of that discreditable story was written while Frere was still at Capetown, Wolseley, proud of his achievement, sailed for home in May, 1880. But Frere's authority in the North was not restored to him. It passed from Wolseley to the ill-fated Colley, who arrived in June. Meantime Disraeli's Government had fallen. The general election in April had brought the liberals into power; and, when the new Parliament met in May, it was soon made clear to Gladstone that the man whom several of his ministers had so outspokenly attacked when they were in opposition could not be kept in office. So, in August, he was recalled. He left Capetown in September, overwhelmed by public demonstrations of resentment and regret at his departure. Three months later the Boer Rebellion broke out—and then Majuba.

It is tempting to speculate as to what might have happened but for Isandhlwana. One thing seems certain. His authority greatly strengthened not only in South Africa but still more in London, Frere would have carried through his policy in Zululand. But what of the Transvaal? Frere was a very able man, far abler, in diplomacy at any rate, than Wolseley. He must indeed, whatever his faults of training or temperament may have been and whatever mistakes he may have made, he reckoned with Grey and Milner as one of the three ablest Englishmen ever sent to South Africa.

Is it conceivable, then, that he might have realised the immediate need of a more wholehearted concession of domestic self-government to the Boers and on those terms, with the swift and clean removal of the Zulu menace to his credit, prevailed on them to acquiesce in federation? If so, the natural unity of South Africa could have been restored and the framework of a united South African nation built up without another twenty years and more of strife and hate and bloodshed. An idle dream, no doubt; for such a possibility, if it was indeed a possibility, perished with Durnford and Pulleine and their comrades under the rocky wall of Isandhlwana.

Notes

As explained in the text, the theory was advanced on the morrow of the disaster that Durnford was solely to blame for it because he had been told to take command of the camp, had therefore inherited from Pulleine the orders to defend it, and had disobeyed them. It seemed important, therefore, to make sure that Durnford had in fact been told to take command and did so, and the point was dealt with by four witnesses at the Court of Enquiry.

Essex and Cochrane, who were both at Isandhlwana at the time, declared that Durnford did take over command of the camp. But had he been told to do so? Crealock, Chelmsford's acting military secretary, gave evidence as follows:

> Soon after 2 a.m. on the 22nd of January I received instructions from the lieutenant-general to send a written order to Lieutenant-Colonel Durnford, R.E., commanding No. 2 Column, to the following effect (I copied it in my notebook which was afterwards lost): "Move up to Isandhlwana camp at once with all your mounted men and rocket battery: take command of it." Smith-Dorrien, who carried the order, said: "On the morning of the 22nd I was sent with a dispatch from the general to Colonel Durnford at Rorke's Drift; the dispatch was an order to join the camp at Isandhlwana as soon as possible." Nothing about command.

In his interesting memoir of his brother (*A Soldier's Life and Work in South Africa*, London, 1882) Lieut.-Colonel E. Durnford says that on May 18, 1882, he received a letter from Crealock stating that his notebook had been 'recovered from the field of Isandhlwana and sent me in England in 1879, and enclosing a copy of the order to Durnford. It is given in the text above. It corrected the version supplied by Crealock from memory at the Court of Enquiry, and confirmed Smith-Dorrien's evidence since there was nothing in it about taking command.

Lieut.-Colonel E. Durnford, who tries to rebut the attempt to pin the sole responsibility for the disaster on his brother by pinning it on Chelmsford, maintains that his brother not only received no order to take over the command but actually did not do so, and was therefore unaffected by any orders given to Pulleine and free to act on his own.

In fact, the question of the order to take over command was immaterial. As pointed out in the text, Durnford undoubtedly did take over, not on orders, but automatically as a matter of normal military routine since he was senior to Pulleine.

Note B

The statement that Durnford gave the order for the company of the 1/24th to occupy the *spur* appears only (as far as the author is aware) in a memorandum drafted by Chelmsford, with the aid of his staff, no doubt, sometime after the event This memorandum was put at the disposal of the Hon. G, French who quotes it at length in his *Lord Chelmsford and the Zulu War* (London, 1939). Part of it supplies the names of witnesses in the margin, and seems therefore (as the author suggests) to have been compiled from the evidence given at the Court of Enquiry. Against Captain Essex's name stands the following:

> At the same time that Colonel Durnford left the camp, a company of the 1/24th under Lieutenant Cavaye was sent out on picket to a hill to the north of the camp about 2,200 yards distant. This was done at Col. Durnford's order.

The official text of Essex's evidence at the Court corresponds closely, though not precisely, with the memorandum, but, after recording the dispatch of Cavaye's company, nothing is said as to who ordered it. The text runs on:

'The remainder of the troops were ordered to march to their private parades'—surely by Pulleine, not Durnford.

Two Zulu Accounts of Isandhlwana
By Bertram Mitford
(At the scene three years after the battle)

The following narrative is that of a warrior of the Umbonambi regiment, who was present at the battle; I give it as nearly as possible in his own words:—

Several days before the fight we started from Undini, eight regiments strong (about 25,000 men). The king said, "The white soldiers have crossed into Zululand and are coming further in, soon they will be here (at Undini); go and drive them across Umzinyati (the Buffalo) right back into Natal." The *impi* (body of men under arms for any military or aggressive purpose), was commanded by Tyingwayo; under him were Mavumengwane, Mundúla, and Vumandaba, the *induna* (chief) of the Kandampemvu regiment; this regiment is also called Umcityu, but Kandampemvu is the oldest name. Matyana-ka-Mondisi was not present, nor was Dabulamanzi. Untuswa, brother of Seketwayo, is the *induna* of my regiment; he took part in the fight, so did Mehlo-ka-zulu and Sirayo's other son. The chief Sibepu also fought.

We were lying in the hills up there, when one of our scouting parties came back followed by a number of mounted men; they were most of them natives, but some were whites. They fired upon us. Then the whole *impi* became very excited and sprang up. When the horsemen saw how numerous we were they began to retreat. We formed up in rank and marched towards the camp. At the top of the last hill we were met by more horsemen, but we were too many for them and they retreated. Here, where we are standing (my informant's *kraal* was situated close to the rocket hill before mentioned), there were some parties of soldiers in red coats who kept up a heavy fire upon us as we came over. My regiment was here and lost a lot of men; they kept tumbling over one upon another.

(The narrator became quite excited, and indulged in much gesticulation, illustrating the volleys by cracking his fingers like pistol-shots.)

Then the Ngobamakosi regiment, which formed the left horn of the *impi*, extended and swept round on the south of the rocket hill so as to outflank the soldiers, who, seeing this, fell back and took cover in that *donga* (pointing to a *donga* which intersects the field about a mile from camp), and fired upon us from there.

★★★★★★★★★★

Note:—These *dongas* are rifts in the ground caused by heavy rains, and varying in depth from two to fifty feet. So suddenly do they occur that where you thought all was smooth and unbroken, you find yourself on the brink of a yawning chasm, which perhaps will necessitate a detour of several miles.

★★★★★★★★★★

By that time the Ngobamakosi had got among the "paraffin" (rockets) and killed the horses, and were circling round so as to shut in the camp on the side of the river, but we could not advance, the fire from the *donga* was too heavy. The great *indunas* were on the hill over there (pointing to an eminence commanding the north side of the camp, above` where the mission-house now stands), and just below them a number of soldiers were engaging the Kandampemvu regiment, which was being driven back, but one of the sub-chiefs of the Kandampemvu ran down from the hill and rallied them, calling out that they would get the whole *impi* beaten and must come on. Then they all shouted "*Usútu!*" and waving their shields charged the soldiers with great fury. The chief was shot through the forehead and dropped down dead, but the Kandampemvu rushed over his body and fell upon the soldiers, stabbing them with their *assegais* and driving them right in among the tents.

My regiment and the Umpunga formed the centre of the *impi*. When the soldiers in the *donga* saw that the Kandampemvu were getting behind them, they retreated upon the camp, firing at us all the time. As they retreated we followed them. I saw several white men on horseback galloping towards the "neck," which was the only point open; then the Nokenke and Nodwengu regiments, which had formed the right horn of the *impi*, joined with the Ngobamakosi on the "neck." After that there was so much smoke that I could not see whether the white men had got through or not. The tumult and the firing was wonderful; every warrior shouted *"Usútu!"* as he killed anyone, and the sun got very dark, like night, with the smoke.

(He is referring to an annular eclipse, which, it is not a little curious, should have taken place while the frightful conflict was at its height.)

The English fought long and hard; there were so many of our people in front of me that I did not get into the thick of the fight until the end. The warriors called out that all the white men had been killed, and then we began to plunder the camp. The Undi and Udhloko regiments, which had been in reserve, then went on *"kwa Jim"* to take the post there. (Literally, 'at Jim's.' Rorke's Drift is so called by the Zulus after one 'Jim' Rorke, who formerly lived there.) We found *"tywala"* in the camp, and some of our men got very drunk. (Native beer, the word is also applied to ardent spirits or any sort of intoxicating beverage.) We were so hot and thirsty that we drank everything liquid we found, without waiting to see what it was. Some of them found some black stuff in bottles (probably ink); it did not look good, so they did not drink it; but one or two who drank some paraffin oil, thinking it was *"tywala,"* were poisoned. We took as much plunder as we could carry, and went away home to our *kraals*. We did not re-assemble and march back to Ulundi.

At first, we had not intended attacking the camp that day, as the moon was "wrong" (in an unfavourable quarter—a superstition), but as the whites had discovered our presence the *indunas* said we had better go on. Only six regiments took part in the fight—the Nodwengu, Nokenke, Umbonambi, Umpunga, Kandampemvu, and Ngobamakosi. The Uve is part of the Ngobamakosi, and not a separate corps; it is the boys' regiment.

The above seems a plain unvarnished version of those events of the day which came within the narrator's actual observation; the following account is that of a Zulu belonging to the Nokenke regiment, which, with the Nodwengu, formed the right horn of the attacking force, and operated at the back of Isandhlwana mountain. The first portion of the narrative, as to how the affair began, tallies exactly with that of the Umbonambi warrior, albeit the men were unknown to each other, for I picked up this story in a different part of the country. After describing the earlier movements, he went on:—

While the Kandampemvu were driving back the horsemen over the hill north of the camp, we worked round behind Isandhlwana under cover of the long grass and *dongas*, intending to join with the Ngobamakosi on the "neck" and sweep in upon the camp. Then we saw white men beginning to run away along the road "*kwa Jim;*" many of these were cut off and killed, down in the stream which flows through the bottom of the valley. More and more came over, some mounted and some on foot. When they saw that the valley was full of our warriors, they turned to the left and ran off along the side of the hill towards Umzinyati (the Buffalo); those who had not got horses were soon overtaken.

The Nodwengu pursued the mounted men, numbers of whom were killed among the thorns and *dongas*, but I heard that some escaped. Our regiment went over into the camp. The ground is high and full of *dongas* and stones, and the soldiers did not see us till we were right upon them. They fought well—a lot of them got up on the steep slope under the cliff behind the camp, and the Zulus could not get at them at all; they were shot or bayoneted as fast as they came up. At last the soldiers gave a shout and charged down upon us. There was an *induna* in front of them, (supposed to be Captain Younghusband), with a long flashing sword, which he whirled round his head as he ran—it must have been made of fire. *Wheugh!* (Here the speaker made an expressive gesture of shading the eyes.) They killed themselves by running down, for our people got above them and quite surrounded them; these, and a group of white men on the "neck," were the last to fall.

The sun turned black in the middle of the battle; we could still see it over us, or should have thought we had been fighting till evening. Then we got into the camp, and there was a great deal of smoke and firing. Afterwards the sun came out bright again.

'Were there any prisoners taken?' I asked.

'No; all were killed on the field, and at once; no white men were tortured: it is the Zulu custom to kill everyone on the spot; prisoners are never taken.'

There seems no reason for doubting this statement, which may be taken as scattering to the winds the numerous absurd and sensational 'yarns' which got about at the time, and are still credited. Several Zulus whom I questioned on the subject all agreed in saying that it was not the custom to torture prisoners of war, though it was sometimes done in cases of '*umtagati*' (witchcraft). Hence it is comforting to know that our unfortunate countrymen who fell on that fatal day were spared the most horrible side of savage warfare, and met their deaths as soldiers, in the thick of battle, at the hands of a foe in every respect worthy of their steel.

GENERAL H. SMITH-DORRIEN AS A YOUNG MAN

Zulu War Experiences

1: By General H. Smith-Dorrien

By the 19th January 1879 the force, consisting of the two battalions of the 24th, one Battery R. A., one company each of R.E. and M. T., and eight locally raised units, was ready at Rorke's Drift astride the Blood River, and, moving forward next day some ten miles, it camped that night on the east of that remarkably shaped and ill-starred hill called Isandhlwana (literally, "a little hand"), erroneously called by some "Isandula."

Some of the transport with an escort did not arrive until the morning of the 22nd. I was in charge of the transport *depôt* at Rorke's Drift, and had been warned before starting that I should have to return there at once from Isandhlwana with a convoy of empty wagons to bring up more stores, so I left my camp kit in a tented wagon at Rorke's Drift.

At about midnight I was sent for by General Lord Chelmsford and told to take a dispatch back to Rorke's Drift for Colonel Durnford, R.E., who was expected there with reinforcements consisting of native levies. I rode back, ten miles, arriving at Rorke's Drift just before dawn on the 22nd, and delivered my dispatch.

It ought to have been a very jumpy ride, for I was entirely alone and the country was wild and new to me, and the road little better than a track; but pride at being selected to carry an important dispatch and the valour of ignorance (for I only realised next day that the country was infested with hostile Zulus) carried me along without a thought of danger.

Colonel Durnford was just moving off with his levies towards Sandspruit (away from Isandhlwana), but on reading the dispatch, which conveyed instructions to move up to reinforce the Isandhlwana camp (as Lord Chelmsford, with the main body of the force, leaving the camp standing, was moving out some miles to the east to attack the Zulu Army), he at once changed the direction of his march.

I had several arrangements to make for transport at Rorke's Drift, amongst others the erection of a gallows for making *riems*. This gallows was some fifteen feet high, and the process consisted of cutting hides of bullocks into strips about an inch wide, working in a circle; the strips then had the appearance of the peel of an apple all coiled up, and in order to be fashioned into straight straps had to be passed over the gallows and through a weighted wagon-wheel below.

These strips were then worked over the gallows and through the wheel, stretched and rubbed with fat until the curves were lost, resulting in very long, soft strips of hide, which could eventually be cut into lengths for tying to the horns of oxen as head-ropes. It is interesting to relate that the first use I saw the gallows put to was for hanging Zulus who were supposed to have behaved treacherously the day after the Rorke's Drift fight.

After starting the gallows, I went up to see Captain "Gonny" Bromhead, in command of the company of the 24th, and I told him a big fight was expected, and that I wanted revolver ammunition. (Captain Bromhead and Captain Chard, R.E., were awarded V.C.'s for their defence of Rorke's Drift). He gave me eleven rounds, and hearing heavy guns over at Isandhlwana, I rode off and got into that camp about 8 a.m., just as Colonel Durnford's force arrived.

Colonel Durnford was having a discussion with Lieutenant-Colonel Pulleine of the 24th, who had been left by Lord Chelmsford in command of the camp, Lord Chelmsford and all the troops, including the 2/24th, having gone out to attack the Zulus. Lieutenant-Colonel Pulleine's force consisted of six companies of the 1/24th, two guns under Brevet-Major Smith and Lieutenant Curling, and some native levies.

As far as I could make out, the gist of Colonels Durnford and Pulleine's discussion was that the former wished to go out and attack the Zulus, whilst the latter argued that his orders were to defend the camp, and that he could not allow his infantry to move out. Colonel Durnford and his rocket battery under Russell, R. A., and his mounted Basutos under Cochrane (32nd), then rode off towards a small hill, apparently a *spur* of the main range, and 1½ miles from the camp. Of the 24th, one company (Lieutenant Cavaye) was on picket out of sight of the camp and about a mile to the north on the main range.

We could hear heavy firing in this direction even then (8 a.m.). This company was reinforced later by two more (Mostyn's and Dyson's), and the three fell back fighting about noon and covered the north side of the camp. The remaining three companies present (for two under Major Upcher, with Lieutenants Clements, Palmes, Heaton, and Lloyd, only reached Helpmakaar on the 22nd from the old colony) were extended round the camp in attack formation, covering especially the front and left front.

Two battalions of native levies were also in this line, but they were not to be relied on and were feebly armed, only one man in ten being allowed a rifle, lest they should desert to the enemy. In consequence of the heavy firing to the north and the appearance of large numbers of Zulus on the main range of hills, and partly, I believe, to support Colonel Durnford's movement, the line was pushed out on a curve, but to no great distance from the tents. Farther than this it never went. Our two guns were at the same time pushed out into the firing-line to the north-east of the camp.

At about 12 a.m. the Zulus, who had apparently fallen back behind the hills, again showed in large numbers, coming down into the plain over the hills with great boldness, and our guns and rifles were pretty busy for some time, causing the Zulus again to fall back. It was difficult to see exactly what was going on, but firing was heavy. It was evident now that the Zulus were in great force, for they could be seen extending (*i.e.*, throwing out their horns) away across the plain to the south-east, apparently working towards the right rear of the camp. As far as I can make out, Colonel Durnford with his force never actually left the plain, but was close under the foot of the small *spur* he originally went to seize.

Nothing of importance occurred, beyond the constant increase of the Zulus and the spreading out of their horns, until about 1 p.m., when they started their forward movement direct on the camp. Our troops were in the positions they had occupied hours before, our two guns busy throughout shelling the enemy. Forty-five empty wagons stood in the camp with the oxen in. It was a convoy which I was to have taken to Rorke's Drift for supplies early in the morning, but which was stopped until the enemy should be driven off.

These wagons might have at any time been formed into a *laager*, but no one appeared to appreciate the gravity of the situation, so much so that no steps were taken until too late to issue extra ammunition from the large reserves we had in camp.

I will return to the advancing Zulus' line at about 1 p.m. It was a marvellous sight, line upon line of men in slightly extended order, one behind the other, firing as they came along, for a few of them had firearms, bearing all before them. The rocket battery, apparently then only a mile to our front, was firing, and suddenly it ceased, and presently we saw the remnants of Durnford's force, mostly mounted Basutos, galloping back to the right of our position. What had actually happened I don't think we ever shall know accurately.

The ground was intersected with "*dongas*," (deep dry watercourses), and in them Russell with his rocket battery was caught, and none escaped to tell the tale. I heard later that Durnford, who was a gallant leader, actually reached the camp and fell there fighting. (Durnford's body was eventually found on the neck with many other heroes of this desperate fight; 130 dead of the 24th were counted there, and amongst them the only recognisable officers were Captain Wardell and Lieutenant Dyer).

And now the Zulu Army, having swept away Durnford's

force, flushed with victory, moved steadily on to where the five companies of the 24th were lying down covering the camp. They were giving vent to no loud war-cries, but to a low musical murmuring noise, which gave the impression of a gigantic swarm of bees getting nearer and nearer. Here was a more serious matter for these brave warriors, for the regiment opposed to them were no boy recruits, but war-worn, matured men, mostly with beards, and fresh from a long campaign in the old colony where they had carried everything before them. Possessed of splendid discipline and sure of success, they lay on their position making every round tell, so much so that when the Zulu Army was some 400 yards off, it wavered.

After the war the Zulus, who were delightfully naive and truthful people, told us that the fire was too hot for them and they were on the verge of retreat, when suddenly the fire slackened and on they came again. The reader will ask why the fire slackened, and the answer is, alas! because, with thousands of rounds in the wagons 400 yards in rear, there was none in the firing line; all those had been used up.

I will mention a story which speaks for the coolness and discipline of the regiment. I, having no particular duty to perform in camp, when I saw the whole Zulu Army advancing, had collected camp stragglers, such as artillerymen in charge of spare horses, officers' servants, sick, etc., and had taken them to the ammunition-boxes, where we broke them open as fast as we could, and kept sending out the packets to the firing-line. (In those days, the boxes were screwed down and it was a very difficult job to get them open, and it was owing to this battle that the construction of the ammunition-boxes was changed.)

When I had been engaged at this for some time, and the 1/24th had fallen back to where we were, with the Zulus following closely, Bloomfield, the quartermaster of the 2/24th, said to me in regard to the boxes I was then breaking open, "For heaven's sake, don't take that, man, for it belongs to our Battalion."

And I replied, "Hang it all, you don't want a requisition now,

ZULU WARRIORS

do you?"

It was about this time, too, that a Colonial named Du Bois, a wagon-conductor, said to me, "The game is up. If I had a good horse, I would ride straight for Maritzburg."

I never saw him again. I then saw Surgeon-Major Shepherd, busy in a depression, treating wounded. This was also the last time I saw him.

To return to the fight. Our right flank had become enveloped by the horn of the Zulus and the levies were flying before them. All the transport drivers, panic-stricken, were jostling each other with their teams and wagons, shouting and yelling at their cattle, and striving to get over the neck (see sketch) on to the Rorke's Drift road; and the red line of the 24th, having fixed bayonets, appeared to have but one idea, and that was to defeat the enemy. The Zulu charge came home, and, driven with their backs to the rock of Isandhlwana, and overpowered by about thirty to one, they sold their lives dearly. The best proof of this is the subsequent description of the Zulus themselves, who, so far from looking on it as a decisive victory, used to relate how their wagons were for days removing their dead, and how the country ran rivers of tears, almost every family bemoaning the loss of some near relative.

When this final charge took place, the transport which was in-spanned had mostly cleared the neck, and I jumped on my broken-kneed pony, which had had no rest for thirty hours, and followed it, to find on topping the neck a scene of confusion I shall never forget, for some 4,000 Zulus had come in behind and were busy with shield and *assegai*. Into this mass I rode, revolver in hand, right through the Zulus, but they completely ignored me. I heard afterwards that they had been told by their King Cetywayo that black coats were civilians and were not worth killing. I had a blue patrol jacket on, and it is noticeable that the only five officers who escaped—Essex, Cochrane, Gardner, Curling, and myself—had blue coats. The Zulus throughout my escape seemed to be set on killing natives who had sided with us, either as fighting levies or transport drivers.

After getting through the mass of Zulus busy slaying, I followed in the line of fugitives. The outer horns of the Zulu Army had been directed to meet at about a mile to the south-east of the camp, and they were still some distance apart when the retreat commenced. It was this gap which fixed the line of retreat.

I could see the Zulus running in to complete their circle from both flanks, and their leading men had already reached the line of retreat long before I had got there. When I reached the point, I came on the two guns, which must have been sent out of camp before the Zulus charged home. They appeared to me to be upset in a *donga* and to be surrounded by Zulus.

Again, I rode through unheeded, and shortly after was passed by Lieutenant Coghill (24th), wearing a blue patrol and cord breeches and riding a red roan horse. We had just exchanged remarks about the terrible disaster, and he passed on towards Fugitives' Drift. A little farther on I caught up Lieutenant Curling, R. A., and spoke to him, pointing out to him that the Zulus were all round and urging him to push on, which he did. My own broken-kneed transport pony was done to a turn and incapable of rapid progress.

The ground was terribly bad going, all rocks and boulders, and it was about three or four miles from camp to Fugitives' Drift. When approaching this Drift, and at least half a mile behind Coghill, Lieutenant Melvill (24th), in a red coat and with a cased colour across the front of his saddle, passed me going to the Drift. I reported afterwards that the colour was broken; but as the pole was found eventually whole, I think the casing must have been half off and hanging down. It will thus be seen that Coghill (who was orderly officer to Colonel Glynn) and Melvill (who was adjutant) did not escape together with the colour. How Coghill came to be in the camp I do not know, as Colonel Glynn, whose orderly officer he was, was out with Lord Chelmsford's column.

I then came to Fugitives' Drift, the descent to which was almost a precipice. I found there a man in a red coat badly *assegaied* in the arm, unable to move. He was, I believe, a mounted infantryman of the 24th, named Macdonald, but of his name I cannot be sure. I managed to make a tourniquet with a handkerchief to stop the bleeding, and got him halfway down, when a shout from behind said, "Get on, man; the Zulus are on top of you."

I turned round and saw Major Smith, R. A., who was commanding the section of guns, as white as a sheet and bleeding profusely; and in a second we were surrounded, and *assegais* accounted for poor Smith, my wounded M.I. friend, and my horse.

With the help of my revolver and a wild jump down the rocks, I found myself in the Buffalo River, which was in flood and eighty yards broad. I was carried away, but luckily got hold of the tail of a loose horse, which towed me across to the other bank, but I was too exhausted to stick to him. Up this bank were swarming friendly natives, but I only saw one European, a Colonial and acting commissariat officer named Hamer, lying there unable to move. I managed to catch a loose horse, and put him on it, and he escaped. The Zulus were pouring in a very heavy fire from the opposite bank, and dropped several friendly natives as we climbed to the top.

No sooner had I achieved this than I saw that a lot of Zulus had crossed higher up and were running to cut me off. This drove me off to my left, but twenty of them still pursued for about three miles, and I managed to keep them off with my revolver.

I got into Helpmakaar at sundown, having done twenty miles on foot from the river, for I almost went to Sandspruit. At Helpmakaar I found Huntley of the 10th, who had been left there with a small garrison, and also Essex, Cochrane, Curling, and Gardner, from the field of Isandhlwana, all busy placing the post in a state of defence. We could see that night the watch fires of the Zulus some six miles off, and expected them to come on and attack, but we knew later they had turned off to attack Rorke's Drift.

I at once took command of one face of the *laager*, and shall never forget how pleased we weary watchers were when, shortly after midnight, Major Upcher's two companies of the 24th, with Heaton, Palmes, Clements, and Lloyd, came to reinforce. These two companies had started for Rorke's Drift that afternoon, but had been turned back to Helpmakaar by Major Spalding, a staff officer, as he said Rorke's Drift had been surrounded and captured, and that the two companies would share the same fate. Luckily, his information proved to be wrong.

2: BY G. HAMILTON-BROWNE (MAORI BROWNE)

Next morning Captain Hallam Parr, one of the staff, came out with orders to Major Black and myself that we were to get ready to march as the whole column was to move forward, so we struck camp and packed wagons. On the general reaching us, he questioned myself and Duncombe as to what we had seen and we reported fully. This interview being over, I was ordered by the C.S.O. to move my men on and clear the road, a rough wagon track over the pass, of any boulders and stones that might be lying on it and was to be supported by a party of the second 24th, under Lieutenant Pope.

Away we went and after a few miles came to a queer-shaped mountain that looked like a sphinx lying down, by the same token I have never seen the beast depicted standing up, anyhow the road ran between this mountain and a *kopje* when we at once came out on a big plain.

I had just reached here when Major Cleary rode up, who directed me to move to my left so as to be ready to encamp, he riding with me, and pointing out the ground on which my camp was to be pitched, which would be on the extreme left of the line.

The column came up, and the camp was arranged in the same form as it had been on the bank of the river, only it was much more extended. As soon as the tents were pitched, and we had had some food, I was joined by Commandant Lonsdale, who had that day come out of hospital. I was talking to some of my best officers when he joined us and his first words to me were, "My God, Maori, what do you think of this camp?" I re-

G. HAMILTON-BROWNE (MAORI BROWNE) IN 1879

plied, "Someone is mad."

The Colonial officers were loud and long in complaint, and Duncombe said, "Do the staff think we are going to meet an army of schoolgirls? Why in the name of all that is holy do we not *laager?*"

In the evening I strolled over to the 24th lines to have a chat with the officers, all of whom I knew well. Whilst there, I had a yarn with Colonel Glyn who was acting as brigadier-general, and would have had command of the column had not the general and staff decided to join us at the last moment. He was a very old friend of my family's and had served as a lieutenant under my father. He did not seem to be in good spirits, but said nothing about the camp and on my remarking it looked very pretty though rather extended, he looked hard at me, shook his head and said "Very."

That night Lonsdale came to my tent and told me that myself and Cooper were each to parade eight companies before daylight, and to clear the rough broken valleys to our right front. He would take command, and that Major Dartnell, with the Natal Mounted Police and volunteers were to act in concert with us, keeping on the high ground. (*Vide The Mounted Police of Natal:* the Zulu War, the Boer War, the Zulu Rebellion and policing the Colonial Frontier in South Africa 1873-1906 by H. P. Holt also published by Leonaur) I inquired if any orders had been given to *laager* the camp. He answered "No," adding language not very complimentary to certain members of the staff, which I fully endorsed.

Before daylight we moved out of camp, and while doing so I saw and spoke to Lieut.-Col. Pulleine of the first 24th. We were old friends, and he chaffed me, saying, "A lot of you native leaders will be knocked over today."

I answered, "If that is so, when I return to camp, I shall not find one of you alive." We laughed and parted. Which prophecy was to come right you shall hear.

At the head of my men, I crossed a *donga* to join up with Lonsdale who was with the 2nd battalion, and on doing so he instructed me to make a detour of a hill and descend into some valleys, he working round the other side in such a manner so as to catch anything or anyone who might be between us.

This movement was carried out and we captured some hundreds of head of cattle, though all the *kraals* we passed contained only old men, women, girls and children.

To a girl, I returned some goats which one of my men had taken from her and, through Duncombe, questioned her as to the movements of all the men. She replied, "That they had been ordered to join the king's big army." We again asked where that was.

She pointed with her chin over to the N.E., at the same time saying, "They would attack us in two days' time." This bore out the opinion I had formed, after hearing the news on the 19th that the army had left Ulundi.

In our next drive I captured two young men and questioned them. They had no goats to be given back to them, but there are more ways than one of extracting information.

They were led apart and well questioned. War is war and you can't play at savage war with kid gloves on. The information amounted to this. They had both left the big army and had come over to see their mother. We inquired, "Where is the big army?" They pointed in the same direction as the girl had done. "When was the attack to take place?" They did not know, but the moon would be right in two days' time.

This information tallied with the girl's and Lonsdale, Cooper and myself discussed it.

The day wore on. The valleys became as hot as furnaces. We captured more cattle. So, towards evening we left the low country after the most trying day and made for the high land.

On reaching it, I at once suggested we should return to the camp and inform the general of what we had learned. This was decided on and as we were then seven miles from camp Captain O. Murray was immediately dispatched, with two companies, to drive the captured cattle there. The remainder of us rested; as the white non-coms., most of whom were on foot, were very tired after their rough day's work in the stony, rugged valleys.

Poor Murray! I never saw him again. He was one of the very best stamp of Colonials, brave, loyal and true, always ready for hard work, a splendid shot and horseman. I know before he went down in the awful hell of the 22nd that he did his duty to the last, and that very many of the enemy fell to his rifle.

Evening was drawing on. We had fallen in and were preparing to return to camp when two mounted men rode up, informing us that Major Dartnell had sent them to find us, and to ask us to come and support him as he had 300 Zulus in front of him, the ground in rear of the enemy being so rough, he was unable to use his horses to advantage.

I requested Lonsdale not to think of doing such a thing, pointing out at the same time that we had no food or reserve ammunition, also that we were seven miles from camp, our white men worn out and that it would be night before we could reach Dartnell, who was over three miles from us and at least that distance further away from camp than we were.

Again, was not this party of Zulus the advance guard of the big army? A trap to catch us or a small party of men on their way to join the big army who would clear out directly they saw Dartnell reinforced.

Duncombe who was asked to give an opinion fully agreed with me, but Lonsdale, who had not got over his sunstroke, was simply spoiling for a fight, so orders were given for us to advance, and away we went.

I regret to say that as we moved off four of my officers left me without leave and returned to camp. Their punishment came quickly, they were all killed next day.

Well on we went till we came to an open valley and saw the mounted men drawn up at one end of it, while at the other end were from 200 to 300 Zulus with very rough ground just in their rear and at this moment the sun set.

I again pointed out to Lonsdale the folly of our joining the mounted men. If it was a trap and we descended, our men, or rather our white men who had been on foot all day were too much exhausted to put up a good fight.

If it was not a trap, the enemy would never stand and allow about 1,400 more men to join the mounted forces but would fall back into the rough ground where it would be impossible to follow them in the dark.

However, Lonsdale decided to descend, so down we went. As we advanced, the Zulus drew off into the rough ground and the night fell. There is no twilight in Zululand.

Here we were at least eleven miles from camp, no food, no spare ammunition, well knowing that a huge army of Zulus must be in our close vicinity. Well, I was not in command, but I begged Lonsdale even at that hour to return to camp. I said, "We know the camp is going to be attacked, every cock fights best in his own yard. When the general hears our news, he will order the camp to be *laagered* and we can put up a fight there against the whole Zulu nation, whilst out here we shall be stamped flat in a minute." But no, Lonsdale would not grasp the situation, and decided to stay where we were, with the intention of going for those few Zulus in the morning.

Major Dartnell concurred with him. They decided to form two squares, our men in one, Dartnell's in another, and we were to bivouac there for the night.

My Colonial officers were furious. Colonial officers are given to speaking their minds. Even Captain Duncombe came to me and asked me if everyone had gone mad. "What in God's name are we to do here?"

The squares were formed. We had in our square about 1,400 natives armed as I have before mentioned, with their complement of white officers and non-coms., but few of the officers had brought their rifles, and very many cartridges had been lost while scrambling over the rocks and rough ground during the day. I of course disarmed the natives, who had M.H. rifles, and gave them to the officers but the ammunition was very short.

The natives were made to sit down in a square, two deep, the white men being inside. Ye Gods of war! as if Natal Kafirs in a formation two deep would stand for a moment against a rush of

Zulus. Sick with disgust, as soon as the square was formed, I lay down and, strange to say, fell asleep. I had loosened my revolver belt for a minute, meaning to buckle it again, but went to sleep without having done so. I do not know how long I slept when I felt myself rushed over and trampled on. I tried to get to my feet, but was knocked down again. I then tried to find my revolver, but was unable to do so. I never let go of my horse's bridle which I was holding in my hand, and at last staggered to my feet.

The square was broken, natives rushing all ways mixed up with plunging horses, while the night was horrible with yells, shouts and imprecations. "My God," I thought, "why am I not *assagaied?*" as half-mad natives rushed by me jostling me with their shields. In a flash I saw it was a false alarm. To wrench a *knobkerry* out of a native's hand, and to lay about me, was the work of a moment. My white men fought their way to my shout and backing me up splendidly we soon quelled the uproar and thrashed the cowards back to their places.

To pick up my revolver and buckle the belt did not take long, and then it was time to inquire the cause of the row. It seems that one of the natives had gone to sleep and had dropped his shield and *assagais*, and this was enough to frighten the bold Natal Kafirs into a stampede.

Yet with *these natives* I was expected to stop a rush of the finest fighting savages in the world!

As soon as I met Lonsdale, I again urged him to return to camp even at this hour, and perhaps he might have done so, when Major Dartnell came over to us and informed us that he had sent an orderly back to camp to request the general to reinforce us. This would be worse and worse, with a force of men barely strong enough to meet 30,000 to 40,000 Zulus, even when in *laager*. It certainly was not the game to break up that force into two parts at a distance of quite eleven miles and just before a big fight was expected to take place.

Again, I sat down, sick to the very heart, but of course I could say no more. Lonsdale was my chief, and it was my duty to loyally back him up and obey his orders.

About an hour afterwards, one of the horses shook himself, and immediately the cowardly Natal Kafirs again stampeded, but we were ready for them this time, and thrashed them back to their places. I then informed them that the next man who moved would be at once shot and that the two Zulu companies should charge and kill off the company to which the delinquent belonged. This threat put the fear of the Lord into them, and for the rest of the night they sat tight.

The weary night dragged on, no chance of sleep, no chance of rest, as we had to watch our wretched natives, and I was very pleased to see the east lighten and grow pale.

After daybreak, to my unbounded surprise, the general, staff, four guns, the Mounted Infantry and I think six companies of the second 24th reached us.

Colonel Glyn rode over to me and drawing me aside said, "In God's name, Maori, what are you doing here?"

"I answered him with a question, "In God's name, sir, what are you doing here?"

He shook his head and replied, "I am not in command." And fine old soldier as he was, I could see he was much disturbed.

As we were speaking, I received orders to get my men into line and advance into the rough ground, into which the enemy had retreated the night before. We were now going further away from the camp; but orders must be obeyed, so getting my crowd under way, we advanced.

After moving forwards about two miles, I found a party of the enemy in caves and behind a good cover of rocks and stunted bush. They appeared to be well supplied with firearms, and opened out on us, making fairly good practice.

I was just going to try to kick a charge out of my beauties, when a mounted orderly rode up with orders for me, which were that I was at once to report myself with my battalion to the general, and that he was to guide me to the place where the general was waiting for me.

Getting my men together and advising Lonsdale of my orders, I requested him to take over my skirmish, and on his relieving me with the 2nd battalion I moved down a valley and found the general and staff quietly at breakfast.

Never shall I forget the sight of that peaceful picnic. Here were the staff quietly breakfasting and the whole command scattered over the country! Over there the guns unlimbered, over the hills parties of Mounted Infantry and volunteers looting the scattered *kraals* for grain for their horses, a company of the 24th one place, and another far away, and yet I knew that an army of from 30,000 to 40,000 of the bravest and most mobile savages in the world were within striking distance of us, and that our camp was some thirteen miles away; left with but few horsemen and only two guns to defend, and it a long straggling camp, hampered with all the wagons and *impedimenta* of the column.

As soon as I halted my men, the general rose and kindly greeting me asked me if I had had any breakfast. I replied, "No, nor had any of my men had any," I might have added "and no dinner or supper the night before." Of course, he understood, that as *commandant*, I could not eat in presence of my fasting men.

I said, "Are you aware, sir, I was engaged when I received your order?"

He said "No," and turning to the C.S.O., said, "Crealock, Browne tells me he was engaged when he received the order to come here."

Colonel Crealock came to me and said, "Commandant Browne, I want you to return at once to camp and assist Colonel Pulleine *to strike camp and come on here.*" I nearly fell off my horse. Could these men know of the close proximity of the enemy? Were we all mad or what? However, I was only a poor devil of a colonial *commandant* and as a simple irregular not supposed to criticise full-blown staff officers, so I saluted and said, "If I come across the enemy?"

"Oh," said he, "just brush them aside and go on," and with this he went on with his breakfast.

So, I kept on down that valley which presently opened out into a big plain, and on the far side of it, about thirteen miles off, was a queer-shaped mountain, the ground gently rising to the base of it. With my glasses I could discern a long white line which I knew to be tents. The name of that mountain was Isandlwana and the time was then 9 a.m., on the 22nd January 1879.

We marched very slowly on, the day was intensely hot, and my white non-coms. who were on foot very fagged. They had had a very hard day the day before. They had had no sleep and no food, and somehow over the whole command there seemed to hover a black cloud.

However, push on was the word, and at 10 o'clock myself and Adjutant-Lieutenant Campbell, who were riding some distance in front, flushed two Zulus. They bolted and we rode them down. Campbell shot his one, but I captured mine and on Duncombe coming up we questioned him.

He was only a boy and was frightened out of his life so that when asked where he came from, he pointed to the line of hills on the left flank of the camp saying "he had come from the king's big army."

"What are you doing here?" we asked, to which he replied "that he and his mate had been sent by their *induna* to see if any white men were among the hills" we had just left, "but as they were sitting resting under the shade of a rock, they did not hear the white men and were caught."

"What was the size of the army?" He answered, "There were twelve full regiments" (about 30,000 or perhaps 36,000 men).

Now here was the fat in the fire with a vengeance.

The big Zulu Army within four miles of the left flank of the camp, Colonel Pulleine without mounted men, or only a few, only two guns, not more than 900 white men in all, the camp not *laagered* and the general away on a wild-goose chase, at least thirteen miles from him. I was unaware, at the time, that Colonel Durnford, R.E., had, that morning, reached Isandlwana; he had some hundreds of natives and a rocket battery with him.

I at once wrote a note to the following effect:

10 a.m.—I have just captured a Zulu scout who informs

me the Zulu Army is behind the range of hills on the left flank of the camp. Will push on as fast as possible. The ground here is good for the rapid advance of mounted men and guns.

This note I sent by a well-mounted officer with orders he was to ride as fast as possible.

The next thing was to try and advance as fast as I could. I rode forward and used my glasses, but everything so far was peaceful.

Just then I met two boys loaded with food. They had been sent out to me by the kind forethought of Lieutenant Beuie of my battalion.

They also brought me a note from a great chum of mine, Lieutenant Anstey, first 24th, who told me he and Lieutenant Dailey had gone to my tent the night before, and as they had found a good dinner spoiling, they had eaten it, but sent in return a couple of bottles of whisky. I was never fated to see any of these kind-hearted men again but it is the fortune of war. Well, these loads were indeed a godsend, and I divided the food and drink among my non-coms. who were on foot and it just bucked them up and gave them heart for further exertions. I would not have minded having some myself, but I was mounted, and they were on foot, so after a ten minutes' halt I again gave the word to move on.

At about 11 o'clock I was on ahead and looking through my glasses when I saw a puff of smoke rise from the hills on the left of the camp. It was followed by another. They seemed to come from a huge black shadow that lay on the hills. Presently another puff and in a moment, I knew they were bursting shells. Not a cloud was in the sky, and I knew that the black shadow resting on the hills must be the Zulu Army moving down to attack the camp.

At once I dispatched the second message:

11 a.m.—The Zulu Army is attacking the left of the camp. The guns have opened on them. The ground here still

suitable for guns and mounted men. Will push on so as to act as support to them.

This I dispatched by a mounted officer, and at the same time my first messenger returned. He informed me he had delivered my note to a S.O. who had read it, and told him to rejoin me, and that I was to push on to camp.

But now my brave barbarians, with their wonderful eyesight, had seen the dreaded foe, and they refused to march. They could not run away as the Zulus were between them and safety, but it took all the muscular persuasion of my officers and the dauntless blackguardism of my non-coms. to kick a crawl out of them.

Umvubie of No. 8 Company helped me at this juncture to solve the problem. He said he and his men would march in rear and kill everyone who lagged behind, so at last I got a crawl out of them. I rode on and used my glasses.

I could now see the troops lying down and firing volleys, while the guns kept up a steady fire. The Zulus did not seem able to advance. They were getting it hot, and as there was no cover, they must have suffered very heavy losses, as they shortly afterwards fell back. The guns and troops also ceased firing. At about midday I was looking back anxiously to see if the mount-ed men and guns were coming up, when I heard the guns in camp reopen again; and riding forward, we were then about four miles from the camp. I saw a cloud of Zulus thrown out from their left and form the left horn of their army. These men swept round and attacked the front of the camp, and I saw the two right companies of the 24th and one gun thrown back to resist them. There was also plenty of independent firing going on within the camp, as if all the wagon men, servants, and in fact everyone who could use a rifle was firing away to save his life.

I at once sent another messenger with the following note:

The camp is being attacked on the left and in front, and as yet is holding its own. Ground still good for the rapid advance of guns and horses. Am moving forward as fast as I can.

My second messenger joined me shortly after this and told me he had delivered my note to a staff officer and had received orders for me to push on to camp.

At 1 o'clock the camp was still holding its own and the Zulus were certainly checked. The guns were firing case and I could see the dense mass of natives writhe, sway and shrink back from the steady volleys of the gallant old 24th.

I had given orders to my men to deflect to their left so as to try to get into the right of the camp, and the officers and non-coms. were forcing them on, when about half-past one I happened to glance to the right of the camp. Good God! what a sight it was. By the road that runs between the hill and the *kopje*, came a huge mob of maddened cattle, followed by a dense swarm of Zulus. These poured into the undefended right and rear of the camp, and at the same time the left horn of the enemy and the chest of the army rushed in. Nothing could stand against this combined attack. All formation was broken in a minute, and the camp became a seething pandemonium of men and cattle struggling in dense clouds of dust and smoke.

The defenders fought desperately and I could see through the mist the flash of bayonet and spear together with the tossing heads and horns of the infuriated cattle, while above the bellowing of the latter and the sharp crack of the rifles could be heard the exulting yells of the savages and the cheers of our men gradually dying away. Of course, I saw in a moment everything was lost and at once galloped back to my men.

There was no time to write, but I said to Captain Develin, a fine horseman and a finer fellow, "Ride as hard as you can, and tell every officer you meet, 'For God's sake come back, the camp is surrounded and must be taken.'"

Then getting my officers together, I said to them, "Our only chance is to retreat slowly, and ordered them to form their companies into rings, after the Zulu fashion, and retire, dismounting themselves and hiding all the white men among the natives. This we did, and although there were large parties of the enemy close to us, they took no notice of us, and we gradually retired out of their vicinity. When we had got to a place, about five miles from the camp, where I thought my white men and Zulus could put up a bit of a fight in case we were attacked, I halted and determined to await the course of events.

During the retreat I had often looked back and seen that the fighting was over in the camp, but that one company, in company square, was retreating slowly up the hill surrounded by a dense swarm of Zulus. This was Captain Younghusband's Company. They kept the enemy off as long as their ammunition lasted, then used the bayonet until at last overcome by numbers they fell in a heap like the brave old British Tommy should.

Well, here we were. The white men worn out and hungry, but most of them determined and I had the satisfaction to read on the grim, dirty faces of my roughs, that no matter what they had been in the past, they meant to stick to their work, do their duty like men and if necessary die game.

Curses not loud but very deep, went up for a time, and one or two of Lord Chelmsford's staff must have felt their ears tingle.

We sat and lay where we were. There was nowhere to go, nothing to be done, we had no food, and very little ammunition, but we had some water and tepid and muddy as it was it was thankfully used as there was no shade and the sun shone like a ball of fire. As soon as I had made what few arrangements I could I told the men to get some rest, as I was convinced that later on, we should be called upon to retake the camp, as through that camp was the only possible retreat for the general's party and ourselves.

After a time, Captain Develin rode up to me. "Well," said I, "who did you see?"

"I first saw Major Black with the second 24th and repeated your message—he at once turned back. Then I saw Colonel Harness with the guns—he at once turned back. Then I saw the mounted men, and they turned back."

"Well," said I, "where are they?"

"Why, sir," he replied, "as we were marching back, we met the staff and the troops were ordered to go back again, so I came on alone."

Why had this been done? Those who want to know had better get the book Miss Colenso wrote in defence of Colonel Durnford, and if they study the evidences recapitulated in that book, especially that of Captain Church, they may find out. I am only writing of what I actually saw myself, and have no wish to throw mud at anyone.

Sometime later I saw the M.I. come out from the hills on to the open ground, form up and dismount. I at once sent an officer to their O.C. to tell him that if he would support me I would again advance. He acknowledged my message but sent no reply, and shortly afterwards he again mounted his men and returned to the hills.

The long afternoon passed slowly away, and towards evening I saw a small body of horsemen riding towards us. On using my glasses, I discovered it was the general and his staff and I at once mounted and rode to meet him.

He looked very surprised when he saw me and said, "What are you doing here, Commandant Browne? You ought to have been in camp hours ago."

I replied, "The camp has been taken, sir."

He flashed out at once, "How dare you tell me such a falsehood? Get your men into line at once and advance."

I did so and led my 700 miserables supported by the staff against the victorious Zulu Army.

We moved on about two and a half miles until we had opened out a good view of the camp, when he called me to him and said, in a kindly manner, "On your honour, Commandant Browne, is the camp taken?"

I answered, "The camp was taken at about 1.30 in the afternoon, and the Zulus are now burning some of the tents."

He said, "That may be the quartermaster's fatigue burning the debris of the camp."

I replied, "Q.M's fatigue do not burn tents, sir," and I offered him my glasses.

He refused them, but said, "Halt your men at once," and leaving me, rode back to the staff and dispatched an officer to bring up the remainder of the column.

I had just halted my men and placed them in the best position I could, when to my utter astonishment I saw a man on foot leading a pony, coming from the direction of the camp, and recognised him as Commandant Lonsdale.

He came up to me and said, "By Jove, Maori, this is fun; the camp is taken."

"Don't see the humour," I said, "but go and tell the staff; they won't believe me."

He had had the most wonderful escape. As I have said before he was still suffering from sunstroke and having somehow lost the battalion he was with, had ridden towards the camp. More than half stupefied by the great heat, he rode into it, and all at once awoke to the fact that the camp was full of Zulus, some of them wearing soldiers' tunics, and that the ground was littered with dead men. He then realized the situation at a glance and in less time than words can tell, he turned his pony's head and rode as hard as he could away. He was pursued, but the ground was good-going, and his pony "Dot" a very smart one, so he got clear away and joined us.

Well, again a weary halt. As we lay, we could see long lines of Zulus marching along the hills on our right flank. They had with them many of our wagons, most probably loaded with their wounded men, or plunder out of the camp.

At last, just as night fell, we were joined by the remainder of the column that had been sent for and we were then formed into line of attack. The guns were in the centre, flanking them parties of the second 24th, my battalion in line on the left, Cooper's battalion in line on the right, and the mounted men in front and on the flanks.

The general spoke a few words to the men and then ready once more, away we went to recapture the camp, or as Umvubie would say, "To die, but have a good fight first."

The night, as we were nearing the camp, became very dark and I received orders that I was to retake the *kopje* at all costs being at the same time warned that if my men turned tail the party of the 24th (under Major Black) who supported me, were at once to fire a volley and charge. This was pleasant for me but of course I recognized the necessity.

The word was now given to move on. At the same time the guns opened fire so as to clear the ground in front of us of any large bodies of Zulus who might be there.

I dismounted and made for the *kopje*, dragging with me the principal Natal *induna*, whom I had clawed hold of by his head ring, swearing I would blow his brains out in case his men turned tail. He howled to them not to run away, but behind them came the 24th with fixed bayonets so that no matter what funk the natives were in, they had to come on.

It was as dark as pitch, and soon we were stumbling and falling over dead men (black and white), dead horses, cattle, ruined tents and all the debris of the fight. But up and up the *kopje* we had to go, for every now and then Black's voice would ring out, "Steady the 24th—be ready to fire a volley and charge." Up and up, we went as the shells came screaming over our heads; the burning time-fuses in the dark looking like rockets. Every time one came over us my wretched natives would utter a howl and try to sit down, but bayonets in rear of them will make even a Natal Kafir move on, and they had to come.

At last, we arrived at the top, no living man was there and as the shells just passed over us, I told my bugler to sound the "cease fire." He could not sound a note, so I shouted to Black that we were on the top and asked him to have the "ceasefire" sounded. This was done and up rushed the 24th, who, when they reached the top of the hill, broke out into cheer after cheer. My Zulus to keep them company rattled their shields and *assagais*, for had not we retaken the camp; or rather perhaps I ought to say, reoccupied it. Anyhow we were there.

Dear old Black came up to me, and on shaking hands, lamented we had not had a fight. He then poured me out a cup of sherry from his flask. I wanted it badly as it was over forty hours since I had tasted food, and my throat and mouth were parched and dry with shouting, mingled I fear with cursing.

However, the Zulus could not have removed all the food from the camp and we were bound to find some. So, I called for my trusty Irish servant, who was a past master in the art of looting.

He was serving as senior sergeant of No. 8 Company and I told him to take some good men and see what he could find. The remains of the hospital lines were close to us so down he went. He was soon back again with plenty of bully beef and biscuits and drawing me aside, slipped into my empty haversack a bottle of port and a bottle of brandy, also a large packet of tobacco. I said, "What have you got for yourself, Quin?"

He replied and I know he grinned, "Troth, sor, is it so short a time your honour has known me that you can't trust me to look after meself." Well, the bully beef went round, so did the biscuits and the brandy. And so did not the port, for Black and I drank most of that. However, there was enough for everyone, and we had a rough but a square feed.

Just as we officers had finished and were sitting smoking, I looked across the Buffalo Valley. By the road it was a long way, but as the crow flies quite a short distance, and in the direction, I knew Rourke's Drift to lie, I noticed a lot of tiny flashes. I called Black's attention to them, saying, "Those flashes must be musketry." He looked in the direction indicated and said, "Yes." I told Duncombe to call Umvubie and ask him.

Umvubie at once said, "Yes, the Zulus are attacking the white man's camp by the river."

I said to Black, "Do you know if the store camp was *laagered?*" He talked in Gaelic for a few minutes. He might have been praying but it did not sound like prayers, and just then all along the Natal bank of the Buffalo huge fires broke out and Duncombe exclaimed, "By God, the Zulus are in Natal! Lord help the women and children." There could be no doubt about it. The fires we saw were the friendly *kraals* and the farmhouses burning, and all we could do was to echo Duncombe's prayer, "God help the women and children." In a few minutes we saw a great flare over Rourke's Drift, and thought that the base hospital, the store camp and all our supplies were in the hands of the enemy. We had not been very joyful before, but now we felt very sick indeed. If the Zulus chose to raid Natal there was nothing to stop their doing so. Our retreat, also, would be cut off. What was to become of us did not bother me. No one depended on me, so I was like Umvubie, expected to be killed but hoped to have a good fight first.

Well, the night wore away. We could get no sleep as we were too crowded to lie down and the *kopje* we were on was all covered with stones.

Just before daybreak orders were given to fall in and as soon as I got my men into their places, I galloped across the camp to my tent to try and save some papers, medals, etc.

My God, in the grey dawn, it was a sight! In their mad rush into the camp, the Zulus had killed everything. Horses had been stabbed at their picket lines. Splendid spans of oxen were lying dead in their yokes, mules lay dead in their harness and even dogs were lying stabbed among the tents. Ripped open sacks of rice, flour, meal and sugar lay everywhere. They had even in their savage rage thrust their *assagais* into tins of bully beef, butter and jam. Among all this debris singly and in heaps, or rather in groups of two or three, lay the ripped and mutilated bodies of the gallant 24th, showing how, when their formation was broken, they had stood it out, and fought back to back or in groups until they had been run over and destroyed.

That they had fought to the last gasp could be seen by the number of dead Zulus who lay everywhere in amongst them, the bayonet wounds on their bodies telling of the fierce, though short combat that had taken place after the right horn of the Zulus had swept round the hill. I had just time to get to the door of my tent, inside of which I saw my old setter dog, dead, with an *assagai* thrust through her. My two spare horses were also lying killed at their picket rope, with my *Totty* groom dead between them. As I said before, my camp was on the extreme left of the line, and the best part of the fighting had taken place there.

I saw the bodies of two of my officers lying dead with heaps of empty cartridge shells by their sides. Both had been splendid shots and I bet they had done plenty of execution before they went under. As I reined up, I glanced out to the left and left front of the camp, and saw heaps and heaps of Zulu dead. Where the volleys of the 24th had checked them, they lay in lines, and the *donga* I had ridden over on the morning of the 21st was chock-full of them. Surely the 24th had died game, but bitter as I felt, a thrill of admiration passed through me when I thought of the splendid courage of the savages who could advance to the charge suffering the awful punishment they were getting.

I had not time to dismount as I heard the bugle sound the advance and I galloped back to my men as fast as I could without trampling on the bodies of my poor comrades. On my way I reined up my horse sharply, for there lay the body of my old friend Lieut.-Col. Pulleine; I could do nothing for him, and it at once flashed through my mind our last words of chaff, so I saluted the poor remains and passed on as quickly as I could to my men.

When I reached them, I asked the adjutant if any orders had reached us. He replied, "No, sir. Everyone has moved off except ourselves and the rear-guard of M.I. which Major Black has taken command of." Good old Black, I thought, always at the post of honour.

Well, he rode up to me and asked me "What I was doing there?" I said, "Waiting for orders." He made a few remarks in Gaelic and then said, "Come on, old fellow. Move off just in front of me, and if these black devils come after us, we will have a nice little rear-guard action of our own."

I did so, and sorrowfully returned by the same road we had so gaily advanced along three days before. A few shots as my officer picked off scattered Zulus was all that happened. But as we crossed some high ground, we saw a large party of Zulus away to the left.

They stood still for a few minutes when they saw us, then broke up and fled all over the country. This was their beaten army retreating from Rourke's Drift. We afterwards heard that they did not know that we had been out in front of the camp, but thought they had killed all the white men. They therefore imagined that we were the dead men come to life again, that we were ghosts, and in superstitious terror fled away from us.

We descended the steep pass to the Bashie River, halted for a few minutes to let the men and horses drink, then moved on to the high ground.

As we came to the top of a ridge, we saw the advance guard on the top of another ridge signalling. I said to Black, "Who on earth can they be signalling to?"

"The Lord only knows," he answered. But all at once a tremendous cheer broke out in front and ran along the column towards us, and Lieutenant Harford galloped back with the joyful news that there were white men signalling from the ruins of the base camp, and that the camp must have held out and beaten off the attack.

Our men began to cheer, and everyone was delighted. We had been very sick the night before when we thought the camp at Rourke's Drift had been taken and destroyed. Now we knew it was safe the reaction was very pleasant.

Yes; it was true a deed had been done by one company of the second 24th, assisted by a few irregulars and civilians, that has never been surpassed in the annals of British warfare. They had beaten off an attack of 4,000 Zulus. True, they had an improvised *laager* of biscuit-boxes and mealie sacks and behind these they had done wonders. But how about the camp at Isandlwana? How about those 900 white men lying exposed to the vulture and the jackal in the camp a few miles behind? How would that fight have ended if they had had a *laager*, and why had they not one?

In another hour we were back at the Buffalo and again lined the same ridge we had sweltered on during the 10th, but this time we only had to wait while half the 24th crossed and only four guns. That long line of wagons that had taken such a tedious time to cross, where were they? They were stranded only a few miles away with two guns and 900 good officers and men.

Well, everyone crossed and Black and myself rode down to the drift last of all. Giving him the post of honour, as he was entitled to it, I rode in front of him, as we came to the water, so that he was the last man of No. 3 Column to leave Zululand— that is to say he was the last living man but there were plenty lying unburied, exposed to the sun, wind and rain, the beasts of the field and the birds of the air, and who was to blame? Who promulgated that book of orders the first of which was that no camp should be pitched without being *laagered*?

In writing this I have only stated facts that I personally saw, and I have tried to hurt no man's feelings who may be alive nor throw a stone at the memory of any man who may be dead.

The 3rd N.N.C. lost 18 officers and 36 N.C.O.'s, only 3 officers escaping. I do not think we lost many men as I am sure the Natal Kafirs bolted very early in the day. I must however make exception of the one Zulu company left in camp. They sat tight until the enemy closed in. Then they charged and were killed to a man. But as Umvubie would have said, they had a good fight first.

It must have been about half-past three on the afternoon of the 23rd of January 1879 when Major Black and myself rode across the drift out of Zululand and proceeded at once up to the base camp.

www.ingramcontent.com/pod-product-compliance
Lightning Source LLC
Chambersburg PA
CBHW021101090426
42738CB00006B/446